The Splendid Art of
DECORATING EGGS

by
Rosemary Disney

Dover Publications, Inc., New York

DEDICATION

To my husband Frank
This book grew out of our love, our interest in life,
and his patient encouragement.

Published in Canada by General Publishing Company, Ltd., 30 Lesmill
Road, Don Mills, Toronto, Ontario.

Published in the United Kingdom by Constable and Company, Ltd., 10
Orange Street, London WC2H 7EG.

This Dover edition, first published in 1986, is a republication of the work
originally published by Hearthside Press, New York, in 1972. Omitted from
the present edition are: the color plates (except for several shown on the
covers), the "Sources of Supply" section and all text references to suppliers.
Added is a "Note for British Readers."

Manufactured in the United States of America
Dover Publications, Inc., 31 East 2nd Street, Mineola, N.Y. 11501

Library of Congress Cataloging-in-Publication Data

Disney, Rosemary.
    The splendid art of decorating eggs.

    Reprint. Originally published: Great Neck, N.Y. : Hearthside Press, 1972.
    Includes index.
    1. Egg decoration.   I. Title.
[TT896.7.D58   1986]   745.594′4   85-20519
ISBN 0-486-25030-X

89629

Contents

NOTE ON PRICES AND SUPPLIES, 1986

The prices mentioned in the 1972 text have been left unaltered in the present edition. Some upward adjustments are necessarily to be expected. Likewise, many brand names of supplies are recommended in the text, not all of which can be guaranteed to be still available. All references to sources of supply, however, have been deleted; you should always consult your local merchants first.

Furthermore, some owners of eggs may still be referred to in the present tense who are now deceased.

ACKNOWLEDGEMENTS

A book of this type could not have been written without the generous help of many people. First, I would like to thank my publisher and the Hearthside editorial staff for their dedication and enthusiasm.

I would also like to thank Sybil Harp, Editor of *Creative Crafts* Magazine; Richard Horkitz of Lord & Taylor; Rhoda Green of J. Walter Thompson; John Murphy of Eastman Chemical Products, Inc.; Catharine S. Dives of *Harper's Bazaar;* Melvin S. Cohen of Walco Products; and Malcolm S. Forbes and William Donald Garson of *Forbes Magazine;* all of whom have been most helpful.

So, too, were photographers Harvey Dresner, Leonard Rosenberg, Willard Dengler and illustrator Carol Nelson.

Next, my gratitude to all my "egg ladies" across the United States: Paulette Bradley; my sister, Priscilla Cowan; Cynthia Gibbons, Hannah Hilker; Gretchen McCarthy; Rachel Playford; Marcia Robbins; June Testa; Adelaide West; and, from Central America, Conceita Llach.

Finally, I give my wholehearted appreciation to those wonderful people, the anonymous egg crafters everywhere. This book is a tribute to them and to the many hours of pleasure they give so many people with their lovely egg designs.

NOTE FOR BRITISH READERS

This book was produced in U.S.A., and to "Anglicise" it throughout would cause a substantial increase in its price. It is felt that readers are fully capable of thinking and improvising for themselves, and would prefer to do so rather than pay more. The following list of suggestions for equivalents and substitutes will, it is hoped, be of help.

Adhesives. See under separate trade names.

bbs. Ball bearings.

Blueberries. Bilberries (blaeberries, whortleberries) are a near equivalent.

Broiler. Grill.

Clorox (for bleaching driftwood). Try hydrogen peroxide, or simply leave the wood exposed to sun and wind.

Cup measures. The standard US cup holds 8 fluid oz (i.e. less than a half-pint).

Decoupage wax and sealers are stocked in craft shops. As a substitute, an egg may be lacquered and furniture polish may then be applied.

Dollar (US). At the time of going to press is worth about 70p sterling, but is variable, as are the dollar prices quoted.

Duo Surgical. An alternative is Eyelure or other good lash fixative.

Eastman 910. Available here. A dual adhesive such as Araldite may be substituted. Evo-stick and Contact Adhesive bond very strongly, but they do so immediately on impact; parts to be joined must be placed with absolute precision.

Eggplant. Aubergine.

Eggs. Exotic eggs must be obtained from special dealers. As to domestic birds, in England many farmers (apart from specialist breeders) rear a few geese for their own eating and will occasionally have eggs to spare. Turkeys are not so widely distributed, but plentiful in certain parts of the country. Duck eggs, if eaten, must be very thoroughly cooked, as they can be a source of food poisoning.

Elmer's glue. Cow Gum is slow to bond, so gives a chance for second thoughts.

Hydrochloric acid. Not recommended for use in the home; only under workshop or laboratory conditions.

Kistka. Try a tjanting, as used for batik. From good craft shops.

Power tool. The "Expo" drill is small and handy and accepts dental burs in addition to a wide range of saws and cutters. An alternative would be a jeweller's pendant drill.

Rit. Use Dylon's multi-purpose dye.

Saran. A clear plastic clinging wrap, sometimes known as Snapwrap.

Shirring dish. Cocotte dish.

Sobo Glue. Copydex is good for fabric. Use sparingly.

Styrofoam. Often sold here as polystyrene. Can be shaped with a sharp knife or hot wire.

Testor's paints. Humbrol or other good paints as used for model airplanes, or a good lacquer, could be substituted.

Zucchini. Perhaps better known as courgettes.

Eggs Through The Ages

"Had I been present at the creation, I would have given some useful hints for the better ordering of the universe." — Alfonso the Wise

EGGS HAVE FOREVER SYMBOLIZED THE CONCEPT OF CREATION. Anyone who has witnessed the phenomenon of a new life emerging through that secret, mysterious shell has watched a miracle unfold.

Elaborate legends surrounded the egg in pagan times. Goddesses of early mythology were often depicted as having been hatched from eggs (perhaps in sun-worshipping societies, because of the resemblance of the yolk to a brilliant sun). To the Druids, eggs were both sacred (if they were serpent's eggs) and forbidden as food (since they were a remarkable source of life). In many primitive societies eggs were used to replace living human or animal sacrifices. In Egypt, eggs were hung in the temples to encourage fertility. In Rome, superstition decreed that pregnant young matrons carry an egg on their person, to ward off evil and foretell (when hatched) the sex of the unborn child.

11

There were many fairy tales about the egg — the most familiar, of course, is the recurring legend of the goose that laid the golden egg in "Jack and the Beanstalk." This story was told, not only in Europe, but in India and in Africa, with minor embellishments. Even our own American Indians had an "egg" story to explain their own beginnings. In their tale, the South Wind catches a whale which turns into a monstrous "thunderbird". The huge mythical bird lays a nest of eggs on a mountain near the mouth of the Columbia river. A vengeful giantess throws all the eggs into the valley where they turn into Chinook Indians. Not all folk stories ended so happily; sometimes the egg was an evil omen or a jinx bringing bad luck.

The custom of giving decorated eggs, however, did not begin as an Easter celebration. In 722 B. C. in China, we are told, an enterprising chieftain — ordered to put out all fire for the three days that preceded a great spring festival — accumulated supplies of painted eggs and dispensed them as edible gifts. In contemporary China, eggs are still used as temple offerings. Early Persians, too, marked the beginning of their religious year with a feast and gifts of dyed or gilded eggs for everyone encountered on that day.

For several thousand years, Jews have used a roasted egg on the *seder* plate as part of the Passover celebration. Perhaps it is from this custom that the egg came to be associated with Easter and the Resurrection (which of course followed Christ's appearance at the Last Supper or *seder*).

Eggs figure prominently in many of the spring religious festivals, although details of use vary. At carnivals which preceed Lent in Europe and in our own New Orleans, egg-based food is traditional. In Christian countries around the world, eggs are painted and given as Easter gifts. In the Eastern Orthodox church, the eggs are painted red, since red is the color symbolizing birth, blood, and rebirth. In Poland, eggs are painted several different colors to commemorate a legend that the Blessed Virgin boiled eggs in different hues to delight the Infant. In Austria, eggs at Easter are painted green to symbolize renewal, green being nature's color in spring.

For many centuries, egg decoration has been a splendid art, with each country contributing its own magnificent designs.

There is the lace-like tracery of Bohemian scratch designs, Ukranian Pysanky eggs that needed one whole day for completion, the embroidery-like techniques of Moravia (in as many as seven colors), the Slovakian flower and fruit designs, quaint Bavarian eggs painted with watercolors, and English pace eggs with natural plant imprints. In America, the Pennsylvania Dutch contributed hearts and difflebirds and the Mexicans used blown eggs filled with confetti to celebrate the New Year.

The egg-decorating art culminated in the priceless, richly splendid designs of jeweler-artist, Carl Fabergé. The first of his eggs was presented by Tsar Alexander III to his Tsarina. Truly beautiful, the eggs were often encrusted with real jewels and always held a surprise inside. Fabergé also designed the first miniature egg necklace. Russian women would receive, from husband or father, one egg to add to the necklace each Easter. The strand was worn to midnight church services. The name Fabergé has become synonymous with beautiful eggs, and his work will undoubtedly serve as a stimulus for all artists and craftsmen for all time.

██

Egg Is All . . .

They say we are
Almost as like as eggs.
— Shakespeare *The Winter's Tale*

BEFORE STARTING THE MARVELOUS VENTURE OF DECORATING eggs, you must understand that, Shakespeare notwithstanding, eggs are like people — there are no two exactly alike.

Eggs are laid by many different kinds of creatures. Fish, frogs and reptiles as well as birds like peacocks, chickens, ducks, turkeys, geese, emus, rheas, ostriches, and quails all lay eggs, so to begin with, eggs are classifiable by type.

Egg colors, too, range from pale to dark and plain to speckled. There are a surprising number of factors to consider when you select eggs — thickness of shells, size, etc. In any case, almost without exception, fresh eggs are easiest to cut. Basically, I use goose, duck, turkey, quail, emu, rhea and ostrich eggs for decorating projects that must be cut with a power tool. Chicken and duck eggs are also useful for inexpensive projects. They have thin shells and can be cut with a scissors.

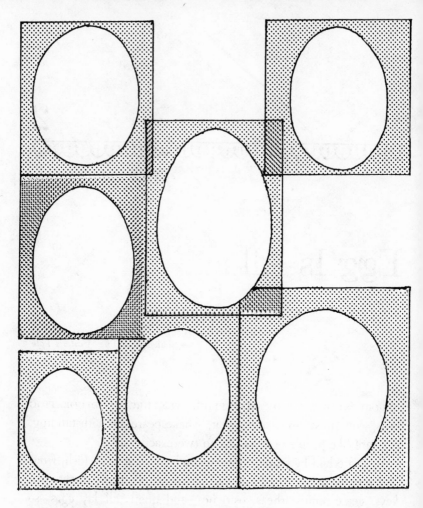

In addition to differences in type and color tone, there is a large variation in shape, as shown.

REAL EGGS

16

CHICKEN EGGS. This is the easiest to obtain year round, and its shell is thin so you don't need to cut it with a power tool, hence it is well suited to children's projects. Use them boiled for

Easter egg dyeing and the simple designs described in chapter 5.

Empty them first. (See complete directions for blowing out the contents in chapter 8) if you use them for tree ornaments. Araucana chicken eggs and guinea hen eggs are also sold cleaned and precut.

DUCK EGGS. I use the duck egg infrequently but, when I do, I prefer the Pekin duck egg, which is easy enough to obtain. Ordinary duck eggs will warp over a period of time—even storage in silica gel does not prevent this unfortunate result. Therefore I use them only for Easter egg dyeing, tree ornaments, and children's projects.

TURKEY EGGS. These eggs are great! The beautiful tan of the shell with the dark brown speckles is most interesting. It is, however, rather fragile, so I suggest that after you cut and hinge the egg, spray or paint it with a decoupage sealer (which also makes the speckling more pronounced).

Turkey eggs are seasonal. You can find them from February until May. The warmer the climate, the earlier the laying season. Buy them ahead, whether you are ready to decorate them or not. After they are cut, emptied, dried and Scotch-taped back together, they can be stored indefinitely for completion at your convenience.

GOOSE EGGS. The best egg for all types of designs and cuts is the goose egg. This eggshell can also be made stronger scientifically by the farmer. The method, not advisable with a gander present, involves adding a percentage of calcium glutamate to the diet of the geese. For esthetic reasons, I prefer to use only unfertile eggs.

The goose egg season varies. Some geese start laying as early **17** as February, but generally they start laying in early spring and continue through May or June. If you wish to keep a supply on hand, you must buy in season, and cut, empty, rinse, dry and

Scotch-tape them back together again, just as you do with turkey eggs. Also sold drilled, blown and precut.

EMU, RHEA AND OSTRICH EGGS. The emu is a native of Australia and the egg is a dark black-green in color with a leathery texture and appearance. The rhea egg is magnificent because it has the truest oval egg shape of all and the shell is a lovely off-white color. Because of its high wax content, slight buffing of the shell will produce a beautiful china-like finish. The ostrich egg is very round in shape and has large pores. The rhea, emu and ostrich are all from the same biological family.

QUAIL EGGS. There are two types of quail eggs. One is plain white; but even more attractive is the egg that is covered with brown and blue speckles which comes from the Chinese quail. This is the smallest egg I use. As you develop your decorating techniques, you will adopt favorite eggs of your own.

ARTIFICIAL EGGS

To people who are familiar with some of the wooden eggs decorated with peasant art, or the beautiful Bristol eggs, the word artificial or fake may seem minimizing (since artificial has such unpleasant connotations). Nevertheless, in addition to the real article, you can buy eggs made of china, porcelain, Bristol glass, papier mache, plastic, styrofoam or wood. Obviously, you can't cut a door in a china egg, but there are lots of ways you can decorate it, and in the appropriate chapters, I tell you how to do so.

18   ### EGG RECIPES

Having been born to the refrain "use it up, wear it out, make it do or do without" I cannot bear to waste the eggs I extract

Plate 1. Never mind that the inscrutable duck couldn't have laid those Pekin duck eggs, she does have a message for egg crafters— if you're looking for a substitute for the more costly goose eggs, use this variety. More rugged than chicken eggs, Pekin duck eggs can be used even for hinged jewel boxes. They are reasonably priced, so can be bought by the dozen for tree decorations, children's projects, and bazaar items. Their translucence is undiminished even after they have been washed, cut and dried. You can order them the year round in two sizes (regular and larger double-yolk) from mail-order suppliers.

from the shells. For those of you who feel as I do, I've included some Disney family favorite recipes, all of them contributed by my gourmet husband who does his "thing" with the inside of the egg, while I preoccupy myself with its shell. Frank, who has the superb palate of the dedicated epicure, tells me that there's no "strong" taste to these turkey or duck egg dishes.

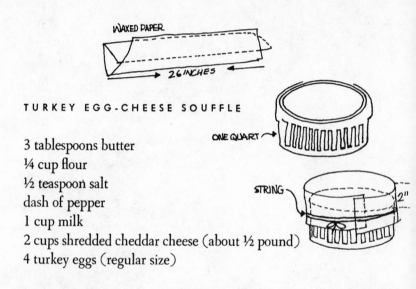

TURKEY EGG-CHEESE SOUFFLE

3 tablespoons butter
¼ cup flour
½ teaspoon salt
dash of pepper
1 cup milk
2 cups shredded cheddar cheese (about ½ pound)
4 turkey eggs (regular size)

Melt butter, stir in flour, salt and pepper. Add the milk and cook, stirring constantly, until sauce is smooth and thick. Remove from heat. Add the cheese, stir until melted. Add well-beaten turkey egg yolks, stirring briskly. Cool slightly. Beat turkey egg whites until stiff. Pour into ungreased 1½-quart soufflé dish or casserole. For an attractive "top hat", run the tip of your knife around the edge about 1 inch from the edge of soufflé or casserole dish. Bake in slow oven (300° F.) about 1¼ hours or until top is firm and golden brown. Serve at once. Yield: 6 servings.

EGGS PORTUGUESE

3 medium tomatoes, peeled and drained
6 goose eggs, medium-size
2 tablespoons butter
3 tablespoons cream
½ cup flaked boiled codfish
pinch of salt
pinch of pepper
freshly chopped parsley (enough to sprinkle on top)

Chop the tomatoes coarsely and sauté very lightly in butter over lowest heat. Beat the eggs, cream, codfish, and seasonings, pour into the skillet over the tomatoes and scramble until firm. Sprinkle with parsley just before serving. Serves 4.

EGG FOO YUNG

¾ cup minced onion
½ cup minced green pepper
1½ tablespoons peanut oil
4 Pekin duck eggs
1 teaspoon salt
1 cup minced cooked ham
½ cup bean sprouts chopped
1 cup minced water chestnuts

Saute the onion and green pepper in one tablespoon of peanut oil until tender. Add the ham, bean sprouts and water chestnuts to the pan. Remove the mixture from the heat and stir well; transfer it to absorbent paper to drain. Beat the eggs lightly with salt, add the onions, green pepper, ham, bean sprouts, and mix thoroughly. Put ½ tablespoon of peanut oil in a skillet over medium high heat, and drop in the mixture, a spoonful at a time, to form patties about two inches in diameter. When they are lightly browned on the bottom, turn them over and complete the cooking. Makes 10 to 12 patties.

EGGS SICILIAN

2 small zucchini (6 to 7 inches long)
2 tablespoons salt
4 duck eggs medium-size.
4 tablespoons olive oil
8 teaspoons grated Parmesan cheese

Score the face of the zucchini with deep cuts and sprinkle generously with salt (more than two tablespoons may be required). Let it stand one hour while the salt draws out the plant's juices, then scrape off the salt and wipe the squash with a damp cloth. Sauté the egg in olive oil. It should be cooked very soft and set aside to drain. Place the zucchini face down in the oil and sauté it over a low heat for about five minutes. Scoop out the pulp, leaving a thin layer on the skin. Blend the pulp with four tablespoons of cheese, place the cooked egg in a shell and fill with the pulp. Sprinkle on the remaining cheese, then glaze under the broiler a minute. Serves four.

This is an ideal dish served with chicken Italian style, or with a tomato sauce and a dash of white wine.

EGGS CHIMAY

4 hard-cooked Araucana chicken eggs
8 teaspoons heavy cream
1 teaspoon chopped sautéed mushrooms
4 tablespoons Worcestershire
pinch of salt
pinch of pepper
4 teaspoons grated cheese (Edam)

Split the egg lengthwise, remove the yolk and save the white cases. Mix the yolk with the mushrooms and cream. Blend the Worcestershire with salt and pepper to taste. Stuff the white cases generously. Place them on a buttered cookie sheet, brush with a little cream and sprinkle with the cheese. Place under the broiler long enough to turn the cheese to a glaze. Serves 4.

EGGS OMAR PASHA

4 teaspoons olive oil
4 slices eggplant
1 green pepper, sliced across
4 turkey eggs
8 anchovy fillets
4 teaspoons grated cheese
1 teaspoon cayenne

Lightly sauté the eggplant in the olive oil; it should be slightly underdone. Place in a shirring dish. Use the pepper to form a ring. Place the eggplant into the pepper ring and lay the anchovy fillets crisscross on it. Slide the eggs onto the anchovy-garnished eggplant, sprinkle with cheese and dust with cayenne. Cook 12 to 15 minutes in an oven preheated to 350° F. Serves four.

Although this recipe is Mediterranean in flavor, it has an African influence.

DISNEY EGGS PIPERADE

2 tablespoons butter
3 onions, diced
1½ green peppers, diced
6 tomatoes
12 duck or goose eggs
1½ teaspoons salt
⅛ teaspoon pepper
1½ teaspoons Worcestershire
¼ teaspoon rosemary

Melt butter in skillet and saute onions and green peppers until the onions are golden and translucent. Add tomatoes and cook until excess juice has been cooked off. Stir in eggs with seasonings. Cook to desired consistency.

EGGS BORDEAUX

2 tablespoons butter
1½ tablespoons grated Parmesan cheese
pinch of salt
pinch of cayenne
5 turkey eggs
¾ cup wine (a good French Bordeaux)
½ cup grated Gruyère or other soft white cheese
4 slices dry toast

Melt the butter over the lowest heat, stir in the Parmesan cheese, add salt and cayenne. Stir until smooth. Beat the eggs with the wine and Gruyère, pour over the mixture in the pan and scramble until fairly firm. Serve over toast. Serves four.

STORING EGGS

Not every craftsman is fortunate enough to have a craft room and storage space for a hobby. Yet, even if you have only a small table top, there are certain basic requirements. The surface must be dust-free, especially if someone in the house enjoys working with power saws and sanders. Particles created by these tools would be disastrous if they became embedded in the finish of your egg.

You will need a storage space for tools, trim and eggs. A box containing small clear plastic drawers is ideal for storing little trims. Most hardware stores carry such boxes, and, if you can't find one with see-through drawers, glue a sample of the contained item on the front of each drawer. This serves the double purpose of storage and orderliness.

As the work area is filled with so many interesting things, it may act as a magnet to others in the home, especially small children, so it would be best if you can close it off with a door. This will keep people out, hide your mess and allow you to leave things resting and untouched while they are in a critical state of preparation.

Additional lights, racks for holding eggs, pegs for holding spools of trims and shelves for storing bases, lacquers, glues, etc., will all make it more convenient for you to develop good work habits.

If you can't spare a whole room, a table or desk can serve as your workshop. Plastic or metal domes like the ones used for party buffets or for cake storage are a convenience. Keep eggs-in-work dust-free.

NOT QUITE ALL...YOU ALSO NEED

These will see you through every decorated egg described in the book. Buy them as needed, however, if you're not planning comprehensive designs of every kind.

FOR GLUING

Elmer's glue
Sobo glue
Eastman 910 adhesive, and bonding solvent
Duo Surgical adhesive

FOR CUTTING

Scissors with straight nose
X-acto knife
Power tool with #9-25115 cutting blade

FOR GETTING INTO SMALL SPACES

Tweezers will do anything that the more costly forceps will do, but if you happen to be married to a physician, as I am, you'll find forceps handy, too. Use either one to place small figures inside the egg on their platform, to reach inside the egg to apply glue in an awkward place, and as an aid in applying braid, or appliqués.

FOR HINGEING AND LATCHING

Hinges and latches for jewelry cases
Jewelry-type chains for jewelry cases

FOR DECORATING AND TRIMMING

Vegetable dyes
Racks for drying eggs
Decoupage prints
Sealer
Trimmings, braids, pearls and beads
Scraps of fabric for appliqué
Testors paints, your choice of colors
Varnish

FOR SPECIAL PROJECTS

Paraffin, beeswax or candle ends
Cords for hanging tree ornaments
Miniature figures, trees, etc. for landscapes and scenes
Sparkle, glitter or Pixie Dust
Ballantine

Card stock for making platforms (save old greeting cards)
Bases
bb's or fishing weights (for jewel boxes)
Stylus (Kistka) for Pysanky eggs

MAKE YOURSELF A DRYING RACK

This easily-made rack is useful for drying blown eggs that have been dyed or painted. A two-inch thick wooden board, about 6 inches wide and 15 inches long will accommodate a dozen eggs. Space long, thin nails 2 or 3 inches apart (or more) so that the eggs, when suspended on the nails, will not touch. Make two rows of nails.

HANDLE TO USE WHEN DECORATING BLOWN EGGS

Buy a spool of fine florist's wire. Cut a piece long enough (about 8 inches) to go through the egg and make a handle. Slip the wire through both holes in the egg, making a small twist at one end of the wire and a hook or handle at the other end. You can then hang the eggs to dry after they have been dipped or painted. Make one handle for each egg.

Such handles would be useful when dyeing eggs, spraying with sealer, dipping in wax or hanging any egg to dry.

MAKING HANGERS FOR DECORATED EGGS

You can buy hooks made especially for Christmas tree ornaments, at any five-and-ten-cent store during the weeks before the holidays, but you can fashion your own hooks, too. Here are three different ways to hang decorated blown eggs.

Step One. Slip the ends of a loop of cord or ribbon through the center of a metal-filigree ornament (not really metal, but it's sold that way). Knot the ends underneath the ornament so the cord can't slip out. Now paste the knot and the filigree to the top of the egg with Elmer's glue and contour it gently (just by pressing down on it) to the curve of the egg. A 10-inch length of fancy gold cord will produce a 4½-inch hanger. The smaller the egg, the finer the cord you can use. It's really easier to do than to describe!

Step Two. If you have pasted fabric or trim of any kind on the top of the egg, you can thread a loop of nylon monofilament fishing line through the trimming and tack the loop in place with the sewing needle. Again, hide the knot under the trimming. This makes an inconspicuous hanger.

Step Three. If you use any trim going vertically around the egg, you can slip a piece of fancy cord through the trim at the top before the top section has been glued down. Knot the cord loop, hiding the knot under the trim. Incidentally, the trim will also cover the holes in the egg.

So, now, on to the basic procedures for making your own splendid eggs. Practice each technique. The more you "egg", the more efficient you will be. While some designs lend themselves to shortcuts, a real egg buff will not sacrifice beautiful results in the interest of speed. After many years of egg decorating, I still often spend eight or ten hours, and sometimes more, on just one egg. But, they are hours filled with much pleasure and satisfaction!

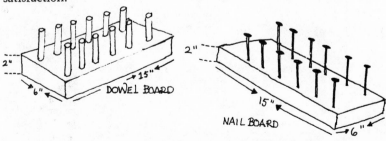

Cutting The Egg For Doors, Windows, Hinges and Platforms

> *"Perhaps the first and last serious problem of building (is) the bridging over of openings and spaces."*
>
> — H. Heathcote Statham:
> *A History of Architecture*

THE EGG HAS BEEN CALLED A PERFECT PACKAGE, WHICH IS, really, just another way of saying that it is an ideal house or shelter for what's inside the egg. Further developing the comparison of egg to structure, I have often thought that egg openings have a great deal in common with arches, the historic means by which all structures are spanned. Like arches, egg openings can be slender or square, rounded or pointed, as simple as a horseshoe or as complex as an S-curve.

The single-door egg cut has the functional simplicity of the most elemental archway which some primitive man might have built for the family shelter, and which was later refined by Egyptian, Greek and Roman architects. Throughout the Near East,

31

wherever Arabic and other Semites (not the Byzantines) were the building supervisors, one can see counterparts of the Mosque egg cut, for always they used pointed arches. And in France many ancient churches display very grand examples of the three-lobed arch of the early French Gothic period.

To show you how many ways you can cut the eggshell, here are some examples of traditional arches. Modify, adjust, adapt and convert them to your own unique needs.

You can buy eggshells cut in any of the styles described in this chapter, and, no doubt, there will be times when you will prefer to do so. However, any real craftsman should try out his skill by making doors, lids, and windows for filigrees.

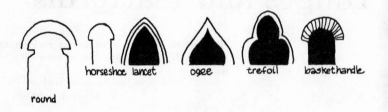

horseshoe lancet ogee trefoil baskethandle

round

PREPARING THE EGGS FOR CUTTING

Step One. Scrub the shell free of all dirt, because soil on an eggshell can affect the painted finish. If necessary, use steel wool soap pads to remove any embedded soil. Dry eggs; refrigerate them until you are ready to cut.

Step Two. Leave the contents inside to help support the shell during cutting.

32

Step Three. The exception to Steps 1 and 2 will be the imported ostrich, rhea and emu eggs which come already emptied to comply with international health regulations and will need only rinsing to remove dust. They will give you no cutting problem because they are hard enough without the contents. There will be one small hole which you will eventually cover either with the base, or a decoration.

CUTTING TOOLS

POWER CUTTING TOOL

For cutting openings in the harder shells, the best power tool in my opinion, is Little Crafty (Sears Roebuck Co.) with the #9-25115 cutting bur designed for it. Do not use a larger bur, because it will not turn corners well. With this tool, I can also change the mandrel (the shaft that holds the bur) and use a diamond-cutting bur. The diamond bur can be found at any dental supply house. It costs almost ten dollars but it lasts much longer than the above cutting bur which costs only fifty-nine cents. The cutting tool should fit your hand comfortably so that it is easy to control.

X-ACTO KNIFE

If you do not wish to invest in a power tool for hard shells, you can cut goose and duck eggs with an X-acto knife. You may have to scribe over your lines several times to get all the way through, and this will, of course, take longer and make a less cleanly defined edge. Cover these edges with trim.

33

SCISSORS

I use a small, sharp pair of embroidery or decoupage scissors to cut fine corners and clip the ends of trimming material — but not to cut openings like doors or lids for jewel boxes. I do use scissors to cut off the ends of chicken eggs or to poke holes in the ends to blow out the insides of eggshells for children's projects or tree decorations.

When I first began cutting eggs, I was concerned about the dust from the shells. After having the material tested, I found there were no serious bacteria present. Nevertheless the powder substance should be wiped clean from the cutting tool before each cutting. A surgical mask and eyeglasses will keep the dust out of sensitive areas of the face. The fresher the eggs you use, the less dust there will be.

THE SINGLE DOOR

DRAWING THE TOP CUT

The simplest cut is the one which goes through the top of the egg to make a lid. If the egg is to be used horizontally, the cut is through the side. You can pencil your cutting line freehand. Or stretch a wide rubber band around the narrower end (the top) of the egg, moving it up and down until you get a proportion you like. Now, with the rubber band as guide, draw a pencil mark all around the circumference of the egg. This will be your cutting line. But don't cut yet.

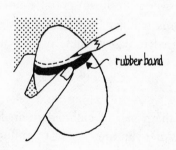

rubber band

DRAWING AN OVAL

(for side cut or single door upright)

A little more difficult is the egg designed to rest on its side. An oval must be drawn on the side that is to become the "top". With a little practice, you can train your eye and hand to draw an oval. Since you can erase any mistake, it's really best to work this way. But if you're happier working with more definite procedure follow these steps:

Step One. Draw a straight line the desired length of the oval. (a to b)

Step Two. At the center of the straight line, draw a line crossing it, as shown *in the diagram.* On a large goose egg, the longer line will be a little over 3 inches and the cross line a little under 3 inches. Be sure that your two lines cross each other in the center. (c to d)

Step Three. With a compass, swing arcs to connect all the ends of both lines, as indicated *in the diagram,* rounding off both ends.

Once you have completed your oval, you can see that this cut will also be used if you wish to make a single door opening, and stand the egg upright.

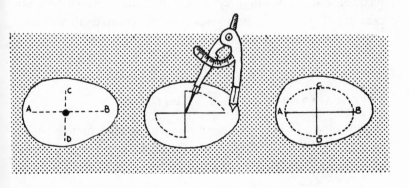

35

CUTTING A SINGLE DOOR OPENING (OR LID)

Now you are ready to cut the opening with your power tool. If you have never used this tool, I suggest you have a practice egg or two on hand before you start the real thing. Also have a bowl ready to receive the egg contents if you plan to use them.

Step One. Be sure you're relaxed and comfortable. Hold the egg in your left hand, with your fingers firmly cupped around it. Rest your forearm on the table, elbow loose or resting on table edge. Take up the plugged-in power tool in your right hand, bracing your thumb against the bottom frame of the egg as shown in plate 2.

Step Two. Now guide your bur along the pencil line. You'll need a firm touch and a steady hand. (Some egg buffs prefer to move the egg, not the bur, and this will eventually become a matter of personal preference. But please do it my way until you've developed your own techniques.)

Step Three. As soon as you complete your cutting, empty the contents of the egg into your bowl. Wash the eggshell at once under the tap to insure a clean membrane. *Caution: Be sure your power drill is far removed from any water used for washing.* Smooth the membrane inside the shell with your fingers to remove any air pockets while you are washing the egg. When the membrane dries, it often has a pearl-like finish which will not peel off. If any air blisters remain inside, cover them with one coat of decoupage paint.

CUTTING PROBLEMS AND SOLUTIONS

Step One. If your cutting wavers, as it may in the beginning, don't throw the shell away. Cover the edges with a pretty trim wide enough to conceal the mistakes. Precision, of course, is the aim of every good craftsman, but that comes only with practice.

Step Two. Since the power drill has a cutting blade that strikes the shell at 24,000 R.P.M.'s, occasionally a shell will shatter. If this should happen, don't discard the shell fragments. Rinse them in a colander and let dry. Then refer to Chapter 9 for directions for making a mosaic picture.

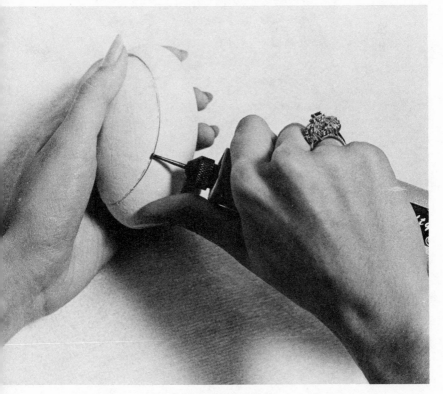

Plate 2. Notice the angle of the tool as I begin a single door cut. I am right-handed, so make adjustments if you are not. Either the tool or the egg can be rotated as you cut.

Plate 3. (Opposite) A double door was easily executed in this large rhea egg. It was a perfect oval, six and a half inches long and four inches wide with a wax-like natural finish. I felt it could take an ornate design. The Polish doll is meticulously and authentically detailed. The costume is trimmed with real beads and lace, and the headpiece is covered with pretty paper flowers. She just about fills the opening, but is not crowded. The double doors were first lined with gold brocade fabric before I added the inside gold cord trim. All openings have the same gold cord edge. To frame the opening, I added Chinese braid one-inch wide and a final edge of rolled gold cord. The finial repeats the lines of the doll's headdress. I made it by running gold wire through little rhinestone balls in gold settings, twisting the ends to secure them and attaching all to a gold filigree. I then glued the filigree to the top of the egg.

Though it doesn't show in this picture, there is a tiny strip of the gold roping, a strip of 1½mm pearls and another strip of gold roping outlining the doors when they are closed.

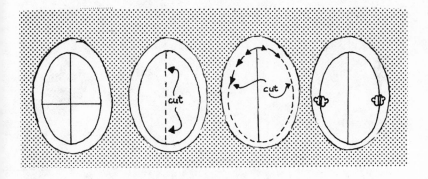

THE DOUBLE DOOR

Once you have learned to make the easiest cut — the single door with one hinge — you will be ready to go on to a few other simple designs which are really variations of the first one.

Step One. Draw an oval as you did for the single door.

Step Two. Cut the vertical line first (this is the line indicating where the two doors meet). Erase the horizontal line so you won't cut it by mistake.

Step Three. Next cut around the oval.

Step Four. Hinge each door separately, centering the hinges exactly on each door.

Plate 4. *This unfinished egg has a door on the front and another on the back so that you can see the figure inside from two sides. Most of the time, one of my double doors comes out a little smaller than the other. When this occurs I choose the smaller door for the front door. This gives better balance to the egg when both doors are in an open position. The figure is a lovely antique soldier which was purchased in the Tradition gallery in London. He is handsomely painted all around and the double door shows this to advantage. Just a simple gold cord and Chinese braid covers the egg itself, and when it is completed, a simple braid will rim both doors.*

THE DOUBLE OVAL DOOR

Follow the directions for the double-door, but round off the top and bottom of the doors freehand in pencil, to make the inner edges approximately match the curve of the outer edges. This need not be precise. Erase the unnecessary lines before you cut to avoid following the wrong line. If you can't manage the curving freehand, try to find a small round bottle cap or even a button of the right size to trace around.

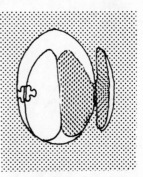

FOUR-PETAL CUT

To make this cut you will need a fairly large goose egg. I use one about five inches long. The widest part of the egg will be at the bottom.

There are several different methods for marking the egg into the parts you will need for the petals, but here are the basic possibilities:

Step One. You can simply draw vertical pencil lines from top to bottom and all around the egg trusting your eye and hand. If you slip, no harm — just erase the pencil lines and make the correction. Or, you can encircle the egg, vertically, with a wide rubber band (wide so it doesn't slip), and use it for your pencil guideline. Repeat this vertical line on the other half of the egg. You should now have four equal vertical pencil-marked segments.

41

Plate 5. (Opposite) The four-petal cut goose egg is only half finished. It will have an oriental theme in every detail. The double seahorse base is available by mail or in department stores.

Inside is a lovely oriental figure which cost under two dollars, yet is dressed in beautiful silk and has carefully detailed features and hair. I have started trimming this egg by adding one row of pearls on the bottom cut, just below the petals. The edge of each petal will be trimmed with gold cord. You can see if you look closely that all the cord has not been added yet. The interior of each petal will be row upon row of rice pearls alternating with a row upon row of narrow gold cord. The rice pearls are planned to further the oriental motif as well as to provide an opulent background for the figure. I plan to keep the outside of each petal very simple, with one row of the same 2mm pearls used on the base of the petals, as an edge around the outside of each petal. With the petals open, this is a very dramatic piece.

In the small photos below I'm measuring the trim needed for the petal, and cutting it off the roll.

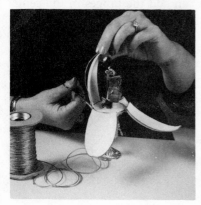

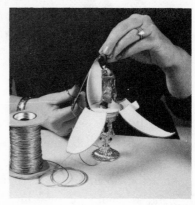

Step Two. Now, divide the egg horizontally; an inch and a half from the bottom is a good proportion, but vary it to suit yourself. Again, draw by hand, or use a rubber band for your guideline, to pencil in the horizontal line. This divides your egg into a total of eight segments.

Step Three. Mark the petals in their present position with corresponding numbers on the base of the shell to help you to reassemble them later.

Step Four. With your power tool, begin cutting the petals from the top and working down to the horizontal line. Leave the bottom parts attached until *all* the sides of the petals are cut. Then cut the four bottom sections.

Step Five. The segments can be Scotch-taped together for hingeing at a later date, or you can add the hinges in the center of each petal at this time.

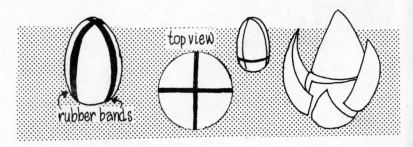

THREE-PETAL CUT

Like the four-petal cut, this calls for a large goose egg. The widest part will be the bottom.

Step One. Encircle the egg with a wide rubber band, horizontally, about an inch from the bottom. Using the rubber band as a guide, draw a line all around the egg.

Step Two. With a firm piece of cord, measure off the diameter, and cut it off. Now fold the cut piece of cord over into three equal parts. Using the cord as guide, mark off your horizontal line with dots to make three equal parts.

Step Three. Connect the three dots to the top center of the egg with three penciled vertical lines. Mark the petals and the base with corresponding numbers for assembling later.

Step Four. Cut on these lines, separating the petals, *before* you cut the horizontal line.

Step Five. Scotch-tape the segments together for hingeing at a later date, or hinge petals to base, placing the hinge in the exact center of each petal.

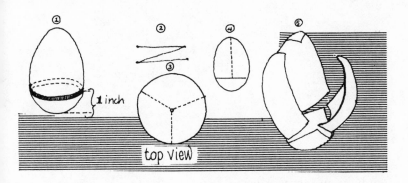

TO CURVE PETAL BASES

Either the three-petal or the four-petal cut can be varied to curve the petals gracefully. Here's how to do it on the three-petal cut:

45

Step One. After you have penciled in the three dots which divide the egg into three equal petals, pencil another mark in the center and about a half inch higher than the dots. Repeat to make three segments. Connect these new marks to the top of the egg with pencil lines and cut along these new lines. Do the sides first before you cut out the bottom curve.

Step Two. Again, Scotch-tape all segments together for hinge-ing later, or hinge immediately. The hinge should be attached at the exact center of each petal and on the corresponding part of the base.

You can make the same kind of curve on the four-petal cut, following the same directions.

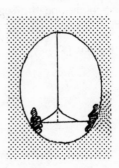

LATTICE CUT

Looking into an object with unexpected openings (remember the holes in Henry Moore's famous sculptures?) evokes pleasure in the eye of the beholder, and the lattice cut box is instant enchantment for anyone who sees it. So many openings! So many little areas the eye can reach beyond the openings!

I use this cut only on the oblong center-cut jewel box, and display it on a table below eye level, where its horizontal design shows up to best advantage. (Conversely, eggs with strong vertical axis are best displayed at, or slightly above, eye level, so the eye is carried up and down the area of greatest interest.)

Aside from my aesthetic preference for using the oblong box for this cut, there is a functional one, because the cut-out door is comparatively weak and gets greater support when laid horizontally. *Here's how to make the lattice cut:*

Step One. Select a fairly large goose egg (no other will do). Clean, cut it exactly in half, and hinge it, as for the horizontal single-door. Now you are ready to start the lattice cut.

Step Two. On the top lid, leaving a margin of at least one inch all around the edge, pencil in an oval.

Step Three. Now pencil in the strips. It is impossible to give you a pattern because eggs vary so. The easiest way is freehand, but if you can't do it, here's another method:

a. Measure off in one-inch squares, marking dots all around the top area of the egg. Then connect your lines until you have formed a lattice. Be careful not to make the lines too close together because you will have difficulty when cutting out the holes.

b. To make sure I would cut out the right square, when I first began, I found it easier to pencil in lightly those to be

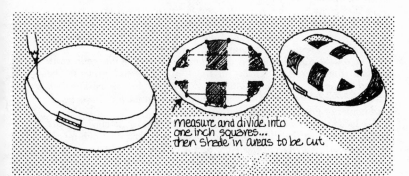

measure and divide into
one inch squares...
then shade in areas to be cut

cut out. Remember, to cut out the squares carefully. If you should break one of the lattice parts, put Scotch tape over the break immediately, then with the Eastman 910, repair it. If too many pieces fall apart, then you must abandon the egg, for too many repairs would make the shell so weak that even extensive decoration will not help.

Step Five. After the lattice top is cut, you have the choice of painting the top or decorating it with gold cord. I prefer the cord because it strengthens the shell considerably.

Step Six. If you use braid or cord, cover the entire lattice with row upon row until you have it completely covered.

Step Seven. Choose an attractive color for your lining, because it will show through.

Step Eight. Select a sturdy base for this egg, for the egg, itself, is fairly fragile.

Plate 6. (Opposite) This is an open view of the lattice design. Notice that I don't attempt to match lattice strips or spaces—it's more interesting that way.

A lattice cut like this is not for the beginner. It requires skill and dexterity and should be executed only on a surface large enough for all the divisions. Working on a horizontal there's less chance of weakening the shell than if you worked on a vertical.

The outside of the egg is completely covered with gold cord, applied row after row, starting at the hinge. I spread Elmer's glue directly from the container along the egg, a row at a time, and then press the cord in place. The only other trim I used are 2mm pearls and halves of flat-backed gold dots.

I edged all the ends of the lattice strips with gold cord. In the center of each strip, three rows of pearls are separated with gold cord, and around the outside edge of the lattice I used two rows of 2mm pearls, again with gold cord between each row. I use cord between pearls not only for added interest, but to hold the pearls in place more evenly. The base features a design of three curled feathers. This egg is in the collection of Mr. Norman Young Gordon.

MOSQUE CUT

This is a variation of the single-door egg. Draw the oval as before, simply adding the point at the top of the door. If you point it too sharply, it will be fragile and may chip. Locate the hinge in the center of the door, on whichever side you prefer.

Plate 7. (Opposite)   The mosque cut lends itself so well to an oriental theme that I carried it out in every detail. The egg is a double-yolk goose egg and therefore quite large. The inside of the door and the egg were lined with a bright Chinese red silk brocade with gold dragons in the design. Outside I used seven coats of mother-of-pearl nailpolish to get a sparkling finish. The oriental figure is of real ivory. After all this, I decided to trim very simply with an edge of gold cord around the cut edges and a tiny row of 2mm pearls. The seahorse base is widely available. Notice that doors can be cut to open to the left or to the right, depending on the placement of the hinge. In a matched pair, usually it will work best if the doors open away from each other.

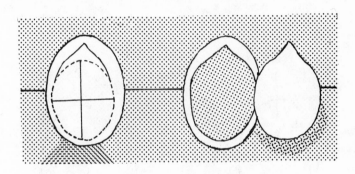

PRUSSIAN CAP CUT

This cut which resembles a Teutonic helmet is a simple yet interesting design. It is basically a jewel box with arcs cut out of the lid.

Step One. Start penciling in a horizontal line about ½ inch above the center of the egg (a).

Step Two. Pencil in a parallel dotted line (b) ¾ inch above.

51

Step Three. Draw two freehand arcs (c).

Step Four. Erase line, leaving only the line between the two arcs. Cut this line first.

Step Five. Next cut the arcs.

Step Six. Erase the dotted line (b) between the two arcs so that you won't cut it by mistake.

Step Seven. Cut the rest of dotted line (b) around the back.

This is a sturdy type cut so you need not worry about cutting problems.

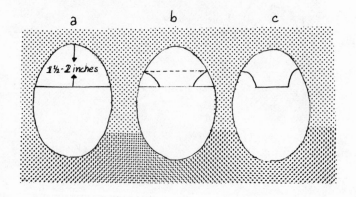

Plate 8. (Opposite) This elegantly simple Prussian Cap cut design might well be the heirloom of tomorrow. In any shade of orchid, it would make the perfect Easter gift. It's a jewel box, with white silk lining. For trimming I used gold cord and 2mm pearls and a favorite gold-plated seahorse base. This egg is now owned by Mrs. Albert Blum.

THE QUEEN ANNE CUT

Use a goose egg for this simple, elegant cut, since the point requires a strong shell. Again, for strength, lacquer is the best finish for this cut and I think the point makes the perfect place for a gem.

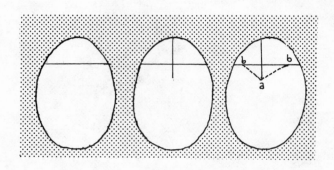

Step One. Draw a center line horizontally on the circumference of the egg, at the point where you want the box to open. Choose between a very small or a very large lid. Do not allow the lid to come below the center of the egg even though the point does. Too large a lid will make the egg look top-heavy.

Step Two. After the horizontal line is carefully penciled in, draw a light vertical line all around from the back to the front to be sure that the point will fall opposite the hinge on the back.

Step Three. From your center line, draw 2 arcs as shown (a to b).

54

Step Four. When you are ready to cut it, hold the egg firmly and cut the point first using your power cutter. If you cut the point last, the shell may weaken enough to break.

Plate 9. *Side view of the Queen Anne cut. An egg similar to this one was presented to Katharine Hepburn when she toured Rochester, New York as Coco Chanel in the play* Coco. *Later Miss Hepburn wrote me: "What an enchanting present—Benvenuto Cellini! It is exquisitely done."*

The finish is ruby red metal flake lacquer: four coats. This time I trimmed the top with a beautiful crown which I found in a department store. It is made by Monet and sells for under four dollars in silver or gold finish, with a red stone. You can change the color of the stone with Testor's paint. Only one row of gold cord was used to cover the cut edges. This egg is from the collection of Mrs. Richard E. Steigerwald.

55

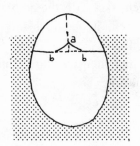

THE REVERSED QUEEN ANNE CUT

For this cut, the point is on the lower half of the egg.

Step One. Start again with your basic horizontal line around the egg. This time, extend the point up instead of down (a to b, above). When the egg is in an open position, the point will be on the lower half of the egg instead of the lid. Refer to the Queen Anne cut for specific instructions.

THE SCALLOP CUT

The scallop cut has many variations, because you can change the number of scallops and the depth of the arcs. However, too many scallops will weaken the shell and make cutting too difficult. Four to six scallops are my preference. Make sure, when cutting this design, to use a fresh cutting blade. This cut requires sharpness and precision. You must change the blade whenever it gets dull so that you will not get fuzzy edges.

Step One. Decide how many scallops you want. I used four in plate 11. Pencil a guideline horizontally around the middle of the egg.

Step Two. Divide the circumference into as many equal parts as you want scallops.

Step Three. Then, sketch in the arc segments. If you do not come out exactly even, it doesn't matter. One small flat area is needed for the hinge.

Step Four. Try not to make the points too severe, for they will break upon cutting.

Step Five. After your egg is cut, Scotch-tape it back together and it is ready to be hinged.

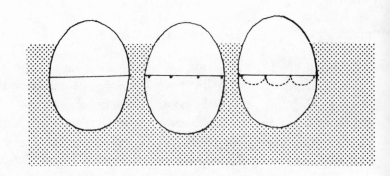

Plate 11. The scallop is quite difficult to cut, but the graceful lines are ample reward for the extra time and patience required. The fine points make trimming a delicate task. Work slowly and carefully. It took five coats of ruby red metal flake lacquer for that sleek and shining finish. The trim is gold cord and 2mm pearls. The base is one I especially like to use. This time it echoes the curves of the scallops. If you wish, you can add a decoration on the very top of the egg. But choose a simple one—it is so easy to overdo the trim and lose the classic styling. An open view of this design is shown in Chapter 7.

THE TEARDROP CUT

The teardrop cut is really a single-door cut with a teardrop shape cut out of one section. You prepare the egg in the same manner, with one difference. As you draw the single door, make a slight curve in the upper left-hand section to form the teardrop, as shown. Avoid making too large a teardrop because it results in a sharp, fragile point. Instead draw a slight curve close to the original line of the oval. If you make a severe teardrop cut, you may weaken the door itself and even lose the fine point when you do the actual cutting. The small teardrop is an effective cut, especially when you paint the door a solid color to make its interesting asymmetrical outline more apparent. Cut the door and hinge it. Then paint the door before you add your trim.

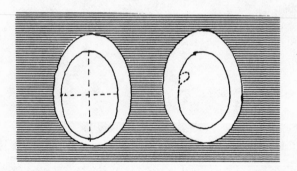

FILIGREE WINDOWS

Filigree windows are a more intricate cut than the ones so far described. They are a delicate way to allow light to enter an egg, and are most effective placed in the back or sides of a single-door egg. The window hole must fit the metal filigree and it can be cut at any stage in the egg preparation. Filigrees come round, square or oblong, and all are very attractively designed.

Step One. Select the filigree and place it in position on the eggshell. If necessary, hold it in place with Scotch tape.

Step Two. Trace lightly with a pencil around the outer edge of the filigree.

Step Three. Remove filigree from the shell and put it aside.

Step Four. Draw a second line parallel to, and 1/16 inch inside the traced line.

Step Five. Cut along the inside line and remove the window section.

Step Six. Erase the traced (or outer) line.

Step Seven. Apply glue lightly all around the hole.

Step Eight. Place the filigree in position over the hole.

Filigrees can be used for more than one window. Two windows side-by-side, and one above the other are shown below.

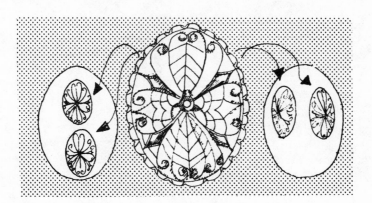

Plate 12. (Opposite)   The filigree in the single-door goose egg invites all who pass to peek inside. This is the closed view of the Christmas egg that contains the Mother and Child modeled in wax in Chapter 11. (The eggshell, itself, has been left natural.) The delicate tracery of the filigree makes an intricate design that one can look at over and over with continuing delight. Notice the row of cord and pearls that outlines the filigree for a finishing touch. The beads around the door are repeated in small round forms in the simple base.

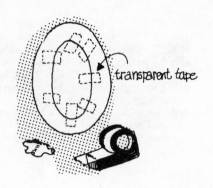
transparent tape

HINGEING

All eggs with doors that are to open must be fitted with a hinge. The hinge must be applied before you decorate the egg. After the egg is cut, place the cut door back into its original position in the egg, and secure it with Scotch tape in preparation for hingeing. Taped eggs can be stored indefinitely if you choose to hinge and decorate them at some subsequent time.

The selection of the proper hinge is very important. Ideally the thickness of the metal should be less than the thickness of the eggshell on which it is glued. Additionally it must have balance, and it must be light in weight. There are many hinges on the market, but I have found those made by Brainerd Company to be the most practical for most eggs. The hinge itself has a long prong, but for smaller eggs this prong can be cut off with a pair of scissors.

A good, well-balanced hinge should work freely, not too loose nor too stiff. The hinges used on eggs cost 4 to 12 cents each.

I use Eastman 910 for securing the hinge to the egg. Although it requires careful application, it has that marvelous virtue of absolutely securing the hinge to the egg forever. At least, I've never known any hinges secured this way to fall off. Have bonding solvent handy in case any adhesive gets misplaced.

Step One. Be sure to place the hinge in the exact center of the door and the matching part of the shell. Mark the placement lightly on the shell before you start. If the door is not aligned exactly it will not open and close properly.

Step Two. Drop a small amount of Eastman 910 on the marked door and shell. You can drop the adhesive directly from the tube, or pick it up on a toothpick and spread it in place. Be very careful to keep the adhesive away from the center post.

Step Three. Place the hinge in position on the door and let dry, hinge side up, for at least 10 hours.

LATCHING

Latches will only be used occasionally on large doors or jewel boxes. The top part of the latch should be glued in position first (this is the part that has a hinge). Then, determine the position of the bottom part by testing it to see that it will function properly; mark the correct position with a pencil. Be certain that your latch is centered exactly opposite the hinge when the egg is *open.*

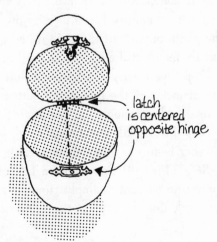

latch is centered opposite hinge

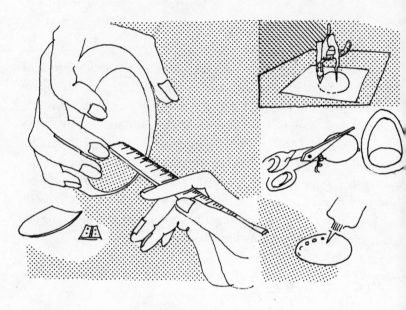

MAKING A PLATFORM

You will need a platform whenever you wish to include a figurine or a tiny scene (or to cover bb's inside an egg). Ready made styrofoam platforms are available, but I always make my own since I prefer the texture and thinness of paper. The best material for this purpose is 20 or 30 lb. weight of card stock that is both flexible and firm. I try to choose a card stock that will complement or blend in with my color scheme. In plate 13 the platform was cut from a brushed gold Christmas card which exactly matched the texture of the brushed gold base.

Step One. After you have cut and hinged the door, measure the diameter of the egg at the bottom of the door by inserting a small ruler through the opening.

Step Two. Half the diameter will give you the radius setting on your compass. Now draw a circle on card stock.

Step Three. If this platform fits into the egg a bit too high for your preference, simply trim off a tiny bit at a time until you sink the platform to the proper level.

Step Four. Apply Elmer's glue all around the edge of the circle, turn the circle over so that the paste makes contact with the walls of the egg, and set it in place.

Step Five. Do not add the figurine until the platform glue has thoroughly dried, about an hour.

Step Six. Put a dab of glue on the bottom of your figurine and set it in place (use tweezers if there is no space for your fingers).

SUMMARY OF STEPS IN CUTTING EGGS

Step One. Your egg has been cleaned and stored as described in this chapter. Now draw the desired opening with a pencil, and cut the shell along the lines marked. Leave the contents of the egg inside until you cut — this helps support the shell and give a more precise cutting result.

Step Two. After the egg is cut, empty it immediately; wash thoroughly under the tap.

Step Three. Smooth the membrance inside with your fingers as you wash the egg. This removes air pockets and insures a clean membrane, free of stains. When the membrane dries, it will have a pearl-like appearance, and will adhere to the shell without peeling. Only fresh eggs are sure to have this pearly membrane.

Step Four. Glue the hinge to the egg carefully. Make sure you don't drop adhesive onto the center pole of the hinge, as this will prevent the proper opening and closing of the door of the egg. Most important . . . let the hinge dry at least eight to twelve hours after gluing.

Step Five. If you wish to store cleaned eggs for hingeing and decorating at some later date, Scotch-tape the door to the egg and store them safely in a drawer or under a plastic dome to keep them dust-free.

Plate 13.   Not one figure or two, this time, but a whole German band, placed on a large platform made from a Christmas card. The turkey egg is a double-yolk but you could use a smaller egg with German Preiser figures or the model train figures instead. The figures and the crest on the back (not in our picture) are pasted in place with ordinary Elmer's glue. The speckled turkey egg has been left natural (except for an applicaton of decoupage sealer to strengthen the shell and highlight the markings). The trim is one row of gold cord and one row of one-inch Chinese braid. The base is inexpensive—brushed gold, short and rotund like the musicians. This egg is in the collection of the Robert Welk family.

GLUES AND GLUING

Use different glues and adhesives for different purposes. There are two main glues and two adhesives for egg decorating, and each has its own characteristics and uses. All must be fresh. I cannot emphasize this too much.

Elmer's glue is water-soluble, so I use it for trims that might have to be removed or realigned. I use it to attach all my gold cords, pearls and trims. Apply glue to the egg, not to the trim.

Sobo glue works best on fabric, so I use it exclusively to glue linings into the jewel-box eggs. The solvent for Sobo glue is water.

Eastman 910 is a marvelous adhesive for hinges, chains and latches. It is indispensable, expensive, and enduring. One ounce lasts well, and for a long time, since you use only a drop or two for each egg. When you apply it, be careful that you don't get any adhesive in the post of the hinge, as this will immobilize the hinge.

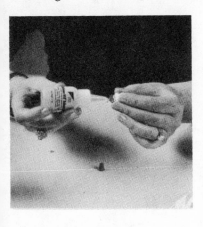

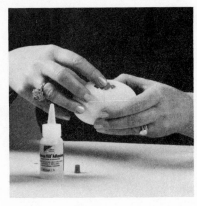

I also use this adhesive to attach the eggs to their bases. Because of its short bond set-up time and superb bonding quality, it is excellent for adding jewels to the egg, whether they are real stones or imitations. Do, however, keep the bonding solvent close at hand, to remove adhesive from the fingers, or for removing drops that fall where they are not supposed to. This adhesive is also sold in a hobby kit.

Duo Surgical adhesive (the kind you use for false eyelashes) is used much the same as Elmer's glue. However, it is not water soluble.

Design

"The artist is born to pick and choose, and group with science, these elements, that the result may be beautiful — as the musician gathers his notes and forms his chords, until he bring forth . . . glorious harmony." — James McNeill Whistler

THIS IS NOT PLANNED AS AN EXHAUSTIVE TREATISE ON DESIGN, but I would like to make a few observations on the subject. Backed by my experience in decorating thousands of eggs, I am prepared to point out some of the design pitfalls to be avoided.

ELEMENTS OF DESIGN

As many of you perhaps know, every material used in design can be analyzed on the basis of its characteristics or elements. Those elements are:

SHAPE OR FORM — round, square, oval, etc.

SCALE AND PROPORTION — these refer to sizes, small, medium, large and the size relationships involved.

TEXTURE — Dull, shiny; patterned, plain; light-reflecting/luminous, light-absorbing, opaque.

STYLE — formal, elegant; informal, crude.

COLOR — natural colors — white, green, beige with brown speckles, and off-white.

71

Of course, elements sometimes overlap, for example, you could have a "roundish" square, or a "squarish" oval; so don't be too hard and fast in your definitions. Still you must make some overall judgments.

Here's how you would judge the design elements of an ordinary chicken egg; it's a somewhat irregular oval, small in size, basically unpatterned; sometimes shiny, sometimes matte, and sometimes (when seen against the light, for example) translucent. Color? Whites, beiges, browns. In style, it would probably be considered formal because of its classically balanced symmetrical form and crisp shape. (Free-form shapes, for example, seem informal.) On the matter of deciding style, the egg also has a barnyard association which implies informal rusticity. This ambivalence gives you freedom to move in either direction when you decorate.

UNITY BEGINS WITH A THEME

The most telling designs are those which create in the eye of the beholder a sense of unity — a harmony and agreement between all the elements. In fact, it's axiomatic that where unity is lacking, the design is poor.

Before you can achieve this homogeneity, congruity and harmony of elements, you should have a decisive idea of what you want. Planning an egg to fit a style in decorating could be helpful. So, although I am against rules for artists (and in my opinion, all crafts are arts if they are properly designed and executed), I shall give you a few basic principles and then go on to a brief discussion of various styles, with suggestions for bases and accessories to fit.

Study the egg before you decide how to use it. To designers working with eggs, each egg is different, despite obvious similarities. The contour of the ostrich egg is quite different from the emu or rhea egg, and your decorations and openings should show awareness of these differences. For example, a slender oval egg suggests a rather feminine design with a narrow door opening. But the ostrich egg lends itself to the more masculine, heavier ornamentation and stands.

A FEW DESIGN RULES

1. Select trimmings so that they have at least one characteristic in common, and one in contrast, with the other design elements. For example, note that I use pearls in many different parts of the design. Pearls are used in linings, finials, edging and highlighting, for the very good reasons that pearls are in every respect but one an embodiment of the egg: they are curved (oval or round), white and translucent. But they have that one necessary element of contrast; their size.

Note, too, that I frequently use a type of gold trim which looks like a series of tiny seed pearls. Here the big difference between the trim and the pearls is color.

2. Be thematically consistent. That is, select trimmings, linings, and figures with your theme in mind. For the oriental design (Plate 14) an ivory Buddha on a teakwood stand is set in an egg lined with red brocade with gold dragons repeated in the print and in the base. The filigree in the rear window echoes the openwork in the base. The door itself holds pearls in a design which follows the teardrop-cut of the door.

3. Eggs are relatively small backgrounds (compared to the canvases and surfaces available to other craftsmen). Therefore, every tiny detail looms big. Try to visualize the final effect before you apply the first piece of trim. If you have poor visualization,

73

make a rough sketch or play with the materials before you do anything permanent to the egg. It is so easy to over-decorate an egg! The rule here is: know when to stop.

4. Yes, it is possible for you to use a material, an accessory, or something which is unrelated to any of the other elements. Modern designers may do this to produce an exceptional accent, but only where its unexpectedness creates an element of surprise which they feel is needed.

5. Imagination, creativity, unity of theme — none of these will conceal poor technique or poor craftsmanship.

6. There must be harmony and good scale between the size of the egg and the trim used: too heavy a braid, large gaudy stones on a small egg, figures inside the egg that are out of perspective will detract from your egg and make it uninteresting to others.

The base plays an important role in the complete design. Because egg bases and stands are made in definite styles, you have a great many to choose from. Some bases are so adaptable that they fit several different styles of eggs. However, there are also bases that seem to me to be absolutely ideal for certain eggs. The jewel box, for example, is lovely on a high base when designed vertically. But, when designed horizontally, the oblong base is not only more attractive, but necessary to cradle the egg.

7. Cultivate a seeing eye and a broad knowledge of all art forms.

CHOOSING A THEME

An egg with a theme is charming and appealing, and if you're planning a gift for a special occasion, the occasion itself often suggests the motif (see Chapter 11).

Plate 14. A brass musician from India creates the
mood for the design. I used alternating rows of
Tiffany-style 1½mm pearls shimmering against gold
cord. Four coats of blue metal flake lacquer make a
sparkling finish for the four-petal doors (shown here
partly closed to make a backdrop for the figure).
A one-of-a-kind design.

Another way to create an egg with a central purpose or subject is to focus on a particular style and, in so far as possible, pick the openings, linings, figurines, bases, colors, etc. to fit the concept.

CLASSICAL

If you're designing in a classical mood, the formal egg and dart pattern or the Greek key are appropriate. Classical themes were popular in many different periods. When Pompeii was excavated in the middle of the eighteenth century, a revival of classical motifs followed, to become the raging fashion. Materials with such motifs (*see drawings*) are easy to come by. There's even a Greek key in braid to use for trimming eggs in classical styles.

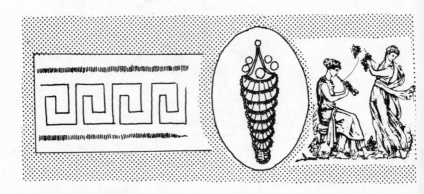

RELIGIOUS

Early art was essentially an expression of religious worship. The three-lobed leaf (such as clover) which was sacred first to the Druids, then to early Christians as a Trinity symbol, was, in the later centuries of the Gothic period, invested with still more spiritual meaning. There is a three-leaf cut which would be very appropriate for eggs meant for religious occasions. Some-day, I'll do a decoupage triptych using this cut, and maybe set it on a tripodal base which is available in gold plating. There's also an ogee arch (a pointed arch which has a reverse curve near the apex) that is reminiscent of the tapered one seen in churches built during the fifteenth century. This cut, too, seems to me to have strong religious symbolism.

GOTHIC AND RENAISSANCE

Inspired by the romantic designs of the late Gothic and Renais-sance period (which persist today in large-scaled Spanish Medi-terranean furniture), you might consider using as a base for your egg, grotesque animals, X-shapes, and richly carved objects in general (including swags, cornucopias and arrangements in baskets). The scale of the period tends towards the massive, al-though classic straight lines were widely used. A handsome base which shows three fruit arrangements in a basket is on the market, and would be a good choice for an egg in a rich and magnificent mood. You can also find a Spanish-style base in commercial pro-duction.

TUDOR STYLES

In the seventeenth century, the Tudor arch (lower and more masculine) replaced the Gothic arch. And it was during this period, too, that increased world trade brought new ideas and new materials from country to country. China and Japan contributed filigreed screens, lacquers, porcelains and jades, Persia sent rugs. India was a source for crewel work, paisley and

Jacobean florals, which are so popular today. I hope this catalog of treasures recalls a special house to you, as it does to me. I am thinking of a rather handsome Tudor (never mind that it's only 40 years old — the archways, feudal ceilings and oak beams are all in the Tudor style). And it has many of the trimmings of the early period, including crewel work draperies, a Persian rug and Tudor arches between all the front rooms. If you are planning an egg for such a setting, a speckled-turkey egg projects the masculinity of the period. Braids, trimming and accessories, too, should have more bulk or dignity than grace and lightness. Then take a look at a brass base (taboret) which seeems to be a series of Tudor arches. It would be a handsome support for such a sturdy egg design. Small detail — but your egg is a masterpiece of small details, as I've said before and will say again.

QUEEN ANNE

Artists owe a lot to Queen Anne. The S-curved cabriole leg (convex at the "knee" and concave at the "ankle") used in chairs named for the queen, is echoed in a commercially-available egg base. It is appropriate for any graceful and delicate egg. In fact, it is the most generally useful of all bases. It fits any type of setting and almost any style. An unpretentious style of lid for a jewel box egg is also called Queen Anne, because it has this convex-concave form.

78

Plate 15. (Opposite) The angel's candid gaze, full dimpled cheeks and broad forehead made me think of a robust German mädchen, so I paired it with the Prussian cap cut and a sturdy base. There are eight coats of ruby red metal flake lacquer for the glowing finish. The interior is lined with white satin. The angel is made of soft metal which can be made to contour easily. I used Eastman 910 to attach it. Notice the relationship of curved patterns—in the wing, the stand and the trimming. The base is properly scaled for the size of the angel.

Plate 16. For a rococo music box design, I used a highly curved improvised base (designed to hold a cut-glass dish) and rather extravagant ornamentation. The ostrich egg, with its large, even pores, has an interesting texture, so I left it in its natural state and added an emerald-green lining. With such a big egg, and the rococo theme, I needed lavish trims so I hung a pearl from each swag of gimp braid edging.

The small music box is glued to the bottom of the egg, secured with glue applied on each corner. The cord attached to the music box is threaded through the hole that is in the bottom of all ostrich eggs (made when the contents were siphoned out). I added a jewel at the end of the string. When you pull the jewel, you start the music. When it stops, the cord retracts.

The music box for the larger eggs comes from Switzerland and is well made and durable. However, for the smaller duck and goose eggs, you can use only the smaller music boxes which are imported from Japan.

ROCOCO AND LOUIS XV

These two styles go hand in glove. Chaste silver, glass and bisque (if you can find them in antique pieces) would be perfect bases. Tortoise-shell eggs that echo Boule cabinetry fit this period, too. There were charming motifs of doves, cupids, shells, Chinoiserie, pastoral figures, flowers, laces, ribbons and palm trees in pastel colors. For inspiration one could examine the enchanting bibelots of the period (some in the Metropolitan Museum of Art in New York). Exquisite boxes feature fine beadwork called sablé, with basket weaves, elaborate gold mounts and mother-of-pearl and jeweled inlays. Keep them in mind when selecting braids, trims and other ornaments for your egg designs in this period.

LOUIS XVI

Designs of this period show a revolt against rococo and a return to classic symmetry and straight lines. Although medallions, scrolls, festoons, ribbon bows and baskets of flowers were still used, the flamboyance of rococo was replaced by crisply-tailored lines. Favored, also, were mythological animals, and Marie-Antoinette's favorite, the swan, was much in evidence.

DIRECTOIRE AND EMPIRE

It's hard to be exact about where the Directoire period ends and Empire begins, since they overlap.

For Directoire, think of narrower stripes, used without flowers, designs that were much more subdued than Louis XVI style and with a trimly tailored look.

The Empire period produced a plethora of bees, stars, and laurel weaths (to crown Napoleon's victories, no doubt). The obelisk and sphinxes of ancient Egypt and the classical motifs from the Greeks and Romans were recurring symbols, too. Again, the effect should be trim, tailored and masculine (see plate 17).

82

Plate 17. (Opposite) This Directoire egg has the typical classicism of the period. From the splendid gold-plated eagle—a patriotic motif of the early Romans also used in the Federal American period which paralleled French Directoire and Empire—to the cameo finial, the design is executed with authentic details. I drew guidelines on the egg before adding the trim. Since the egg texture was exceptionally luminous, I left it in its natural white. Note how the lines of the pearl trim elongate the design. Gold cord outlines each row of pearls.

ORIENTAL THEMES

From the time when trading ships carried cargo freely around the world, Chinese and Japanese motifs have been widely mixed in with all styles and periods of decoration. Chinoiserie (Chinese decoration as interpreted by an eighteenth century Frenchman) used tortoise shells, mother-of-pearl, ivory, and lacquering (known then as japanning). Today's oriental theme could be expressed with lovely miniature Buddhas and ivory and jade figurines in reproductions as well as antiques. Fabrics and stands to go with the oriental theme are available too. Related to Chinoiserie is

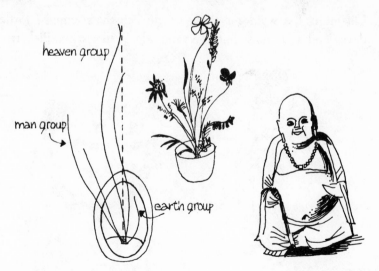

heaven group

man group

earth group

83

Singerie, a style of decoration featuring monkeys in fantasy situations as, for example, plated in gold and holding a place for an egg!

The Japanese heaven-man-earth philosophy of art is based on the use of three basic lines — high, medium, and low. I've shown this in a drawing that could be used as a dried-flower appliqué. Since the Japanese stress nature, the base might be driftwood, but a base sold as Oriental style (it is!) or Tree Trunk Holder would be equally appropriate, if somewhat more formal.

Speaking of heaven-man-earth lines, did you know that eggs were revered as a sacred symbol in ancient times? The egg represented the world and its elements: shell (earth), white (water), yolk (fire), and, under the shell, air.

VICTORIAN

Quaint is the word for those ornate bowknots, cupids, turtle-doves and what-nots—but everyone adores this style. Pick trim

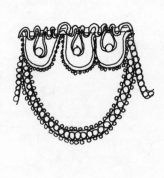

edging a little too big for the egg, find a base with a little too much carving, add lots of mother-of-pearl, you may even be lucky enough to find a Parian hand vase to hold the egg — and chances are the result will be Victorian.

FOLK ART

Egging began as a peasant art and some of the most dedicated eggers prefer this type of decoration. Turn for inspiration to colorful folk designs in America and in countries all over the world. The literature on folk art is abundant. It could be French Provincial, Pennsylvania Dutch, Shaker, Italian peasant, Early American, Indian, Scandinavian, Spanish or English cottage, but it is always sturdy, often naive and informal, and usually done with bright clear primary colors. Look for small dolls in regional costumes, and animals to use as bases, figurines, etc. You can even find Polish folk tunes in tiny music boxes to fit your egg and make it a musical one.

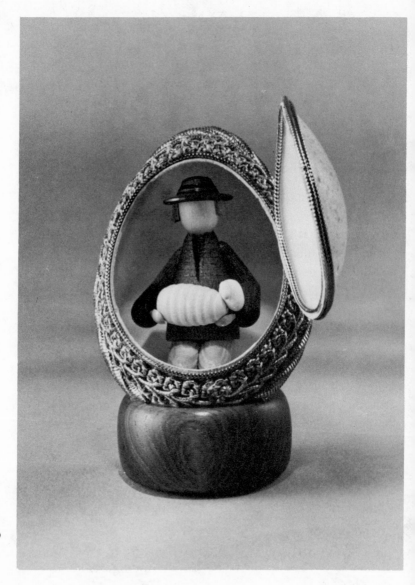

Plate 18. (Opposite)   Almost all-monochromatic in color, this egg depends, for interest, on a variety of textures. The turkey egg, with its single door, is beige with brown speckles. The Polish peasant figure is in several kinds of wood (no platform needed for this) and the base is a wooden napkin ring. Gold cord and wide trim outline the oval of the opening. Gold cord also outlines the edge of the door. There are just three of these eggs. One is in the collection of Mrs. Robert Peterson, the second of Mrs. Robert Welk, and the third of the author.

THE ECLECTIC DECORATOR

Frank Lloyd Wright defined an eclectic as a man "guided only by instinct of choice called 'taste'." That is to say, a man who understood the nature of design and used his rich imagination and sense of fitness to guide his artistry, rather than blindly following "traditional styles."

And here, my friends, is the best advice anyone can give you: do, by all means, know history, but in the final analysis, make use of that instinct called "taste" to guide your hands and imagination.

5

Decorating The Shell

> "The three most universally admired gifts of
> the orient, Japan and China, to the west are silk,
> porcelain, and lacquer. Besides lacquer, the in-
> gredient essential to the entirely texture-free look
> of translucent color-in-depth of fine lacquer ware
> is patience."   — Michael Greer, *Inside Design*

WHETHER YOU'RE DECORATING EGGS FOR THE CHILDREN OR
making a gift you hope will become an heirloom, read the section
on design before you decide how to decorate the shell. A carefully planned design plus painstaking workmanship and good
working materials is the combination that results in splendid eggs.

All sorts of ornaments and finishes may be used to decorate an
eggshell. In this chapter, I have included the least complicated
decorations, such as appliqué and collage, as well as the breath-
takingly beautiful lacquer finishes that can only be achieved by
a patient craftsman. The famous Fabergé look was achieved with
such a finish. You'll also find out how to work with real gold
leaf, decoupage and how to apply a fine porcelain finish. If you
like fast results, you'll want to try etching on a plain egg, or
marbleizing the one-dip way. Batik is a dip method, too, but
it takes a little longer. Pearlizing can be done two ways — the
quickie way with nailpolish, or the slow way with real mother-of-
pearl.

Are you wondering what the difference is between appliqué, collage and decoupage? Most people find their resemblances confusing.

With appliqué, you fasten or paste one or more shapes to a larger shape or background. Fabrics, braids, beads, flowers are the smaller shapes which you apply to the larger background (the egg) to conceal an edge, or ornament the design. Enchanting though the results may be, appliqué is not a complicated procedure.

With collage, you overlap materials (tissue paper, string, fabric, etc.), rather as the Cubists did, to represent changes in plane and texture, pasting them down in effects that please your eye but are not inordinately difficult to accomplish.

But of the three cousinly crafts, decoupage is the most masterful of all. You cut out and paste down (usually reassembled) designs, and when you've finished, you have created the illusion that the paper is "sunk" into the egg. This you do with exquisite patience by adding layer after layer of clear lacquer, building up the surface of the egg to the level of the paper you pasted to it.

All of these basic processes, as well as others, are described in detail under their various headings. But as any good chef knows, it's one thing to read a cookbook and quite another to sit down to the recipes. My first "recipe" is for appliqué because it happens to be under the first letter of the alphabet, but it's also the easiest form of decoration to do and to do it you must first learn to boil an egg.

APPLIQUE

The appliqué material can be almost anything: a wisp of fabric, a few seeds or beads, several scraps of fabrics applied in random patchwork-style, braid, sequins, spangles, paper (flocked, foil, tissue, etc.) moving eyes (for making faces on eggs), tassels, gold medallions, felt, lace, feathers, even small butterflies. The range is limited only by what you can find in the store, in your scrap bag, or in your own backyard.

The materials can be used in many different styles. For example, in Germany and Poland, appliqués are often attached to the decorated egg so that they resemble a pitcher, with the pouring spout and handle made of stiff paper.

Appliqué does not take much time or skill, nor does it need the hard shell required for the more elegant effects. I use appliqué designs for ornamenting eggs for the holidays and for children's projects. Hard-boiled chicken eggs are fine, and they are durable enough for children to handle. But you could also use clean, blown eggs if they are to be tree ornaments.

Step One. If you're using a chicken egg, here's that "recipe" I promised you. Set eggs out to reach room temperature before boiling them; it cuts down on cracking. Cover them with cold water and cook for 15 minutes at moderate heat. Plunge them into cold water to cool quickly and wipe dry.

Step Two. If you wish to ornament dyed eggs, the coloring should be done before you begin the appliqué. (See page 100 on coloring eggs).

Step Three. You can also appliqué directly on the clean egg. Apply Elmer's glue directly on the eggshell, not on the appliqué. Use glue even if you are using appliqués that have their own adhesive . . . it will form a more durable bond.

Step Four. When using plant materials or butterflies, choose small items. See section on techniques of drying natural materials, at the end of this chapter.

Plate 19. (Opposite) Seeing the handsome results, who could believe that appliqué is so easy to do! Make eggs like this in quantity for the next bazaar. I appliquéd real pheasant feathers, but you might find other appropriate feathers in hobby shops, at notion counters or flower supply shops. Inside is a miniature carved pheasant, painted in its natural colors. The edges are trimmed with gold cord and the base is simple and inexpensive. Black and white quail feathers and a black base would have been equally effective.

The smaller egg comes from a South American chicken called an araucana. It will make a welcome gift for collectors of all things miniature. The tiny single door is painted blue and trimmed with gold cord, 2mm pearls and bullion. I repeated this trim on the egg opening. I made a platform to hold the tiny wooden angel and used an inexpensive base.

93

BALLANTINE

You can find a material called *ballantine* at some craft or hobby shops. It consists of tiny crystals that can be sprinkled on the egg to add texture. Use it with care; it tends to scatter. This is an excellent material for decorating eggs for Christmas trees or other holiday festivities.

Step One. Coat an entire blown egg with Elmer's glue, applying it with a paintbrush.

Step Two. While the egg is still tacky, gently pour the ballantine all over it, letting the excess fall into a box lid so that you can reuse it. The ballantine will give the shell a translucent look. Use it inside the lids of jewel boxes, or inside the door of an egg that opens, for a change from fabric lining.

BATIK OR WAX-RESIST

Batik was first used by the Indonesians as a method of dyeing cloth. It is a method of hand-printing by coating parts of a surface with wax to resist dye, dipping it in a cold dye solution, and boiling off the wax. The process is repeated as many times as there are colors in the design. The method is easily adapted to decorating eggs. Any size egg can be used, provided that the contents have been blown out. This is the way it's done:

Step One. Heat paraffin wax in a tin can set in a larger can or vessel of boiling water. Never heat wax directly on the burner — it may spatter and burn you. One pound of wax will be enough for at least 3 dozen chicken eggs.

Step Two. Dip the eggshell in wax, using hibachi sticks. Or use a fine florist's wire that has been slipped through the holes you made by emptying the egg. Loop the end of the wire to make a dipping "handle". Make a new wire handle for each egg.

Step Three. Cool the egg for 10 minutes to set wax. Then, holding the egg, cut a design into the wax with a large darning needle or stylus.

Step Four. Prepare one or more commercial vegetable colors as directed by the manufacturer. Then dip the egg into one of these vegetable dyes.

Step Five. Remove from dye bath and dip in vinegar to set the color.

Step Six. Immerse the egg in boiling water to remove the wax. The colored design will remain on the shell. Wherever there was a wax coating, there will be no color.

Step Seven. Repeat the entire process from step 2 to step 6 as often as you wish, adding a new color each time. Remember that yellow over blue will produce green, red over blue will make purple, and yellow over red will make orange. Also, it is best to progress from light to dark colors; that is, dip your egg in the lighter tints first. Keep this in mind when you plan your design.

Step Eight. Polish the eggs with a cloth and a little vegetable oil.

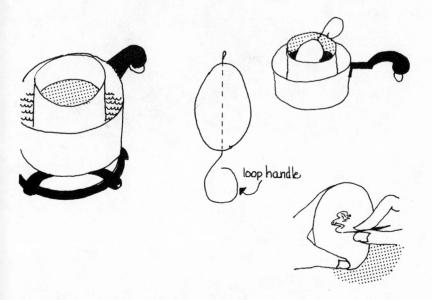

loop handle

COLLAGE

The art of combining, overlapping or arranging bits of paper on a background, called collage, is quite adaptable to egg decorating. Once again, the egg is the background.

Tissue paper, flocked paper, in fact, almost any pretty paper that comes to hand, can be used for collage if it is not too heavy. Thinner papers will conform to the egg shape best. Lace paper is especially useful.

Step One. Collage can be applied to a plain egg or a painted one. Do your painting first, and dry it thoroughly before you start the collage.

Step Two. Cut an assortment of interesting shapes and arrange them on a piece of paper so that you can re-arrange until you get a design that will both fit the egg and please you. Try flowers with overlays to suggest petals in depth, miniature figures from a print (of course the figures must be small enough to fit the egg) or abstract designs.

Step Three. An alternate to a design with paper bits might be a photograph or a magazine cutout combined with letters clipped from a magazine.

Step Four. Apply paste to the egg if your material is flimsy; apply paste to the paper, if the cutout is firm. Use Elmer's glue and be sure to apply the underlays *first.* If the material you clip is a bit heavy, use the Eastman 910 to glue it down, or peel off some of the backing.

Step Five. Spray the finished collage with fixative.

DECOUPAGE

Hiram Manning, the great world authority on the subject, says in his book, *Manning on Decoupage,* that the modern version of decoupage was introduced in Venice in the eighteenth century. In the hands of the Venetian designers, it was an elaborate technique developed to imitate hand-painted furniture. Ornate and complex designs were cut from engravings, and the cutouts were then glued to the background and "sunk" deeply into the wood under many coats of varnish.

Compared with this kind of decoupage, decorating an egg (whole or blown) with paper cutouts will seem to be an easy job. Choose a properly scaled print or engraving, or use only part of a larger picture. Don't crop the picture at a point of interest; don't design it so that you have to turn the egg in order to see the whole picture. Be sure the design will be attractive from any angle as you turn the egg around. If you have a favorite picture, such as a Jean Pillement print sold for decoupage, you might be able to use part of it. If you can't come by anything so authentically eighteenth century, magazine prints should not be overlooked. Simply paint the wrong side of the print with decoupage paint so the colors won't bleed. If you paint well, you might choose a black and white print and color it yourself.

If you should acquire a print on heavy or thick paper, you can often peel it to make it thin enough to use for decoupage. Moisten, but don't soak, the back with white vinegar. Let it stand for a minute, then rub off the excess paper with a damp sponge or your fingers. It may not work, but it's worth a try. When dry, apply decoupage sealer on top.

METHOD:

Step One. Plan your design on paper where you can still make changes.

*Reprinted by Dover, 24028-2.

Step Two. Wash the egg thoroughly, and dry.

Step Three. Cut out the picture that is to be used. Test it against the curve of the egg. If you think you will have trouble making it contour, make tiny nips all around the edges with the scissors.

Step Four. You can apply decoupage sealer to the egg at this time, but I, personally, do not.

Step Five. Using Elmer's glue thinned with a little water, apply the glue to the back of the picture, not the egg. This does not allow you the freedom of moving the print, as in true decoupage fashion (when the whole surface is glued) so be sure you know where you want to place your print. Now press the print on the egg.

Step Six. Let the picture dry. Then check to be sure all ends are secure. If not, spread glue on a toothpick, then onto the loose ends.

Step Seven. When all ends are secure, apply just one coat of decoupage sealer.

Step Eight. Allow four to six hours for the sealer to dry. Then begin applying your clear lacquer or varnish finish, allowing overnight for drying between coats.

Step Nine. Five or six coats will make a very good finish. However, if you want a true decoupage look, with the design appearing to be sunk deep in the shell, you may have to apply as many as fifteen coats. Because of the delicacy of the egg, sanding is not recommended. Unless you use a blown egg which can be dried on a rack, you cannot lacquer the whole egg and lay it down to dry, therefore, you will have to do it in sections. It is not easy to avoid showing a start-and-finish line, or buildup where you don't want it. Try to find places to end off where it will show the least.

Step Ten. As a final step, wax the finished product using decoupage wax. It will add a beautiful satin-like matte finish.

99

Note: If you want to decoupage a colored egg, use decoupage paint only, and apply it as your first step.

DYEING EGGS

TO MAKE YOUR OWN NATURAL DYES

Beautiful colors can be made from vegetables and vegetable skins, and with so much interest in ecology I thought you'd like to know how to use them. If you use a larger quantity of vegetables you get a stronger color. A few drops of vinegar are added to make colors last longer. These are the directions:

YELLOW: Cook the skins from ½ dozen large onions in 1½ cups water. Do not season. Time as usual for cooking the vegetable, and drain off the water. If you do not use it immediately, it must be reheated to just below a boil for dyeing purposes. You also get a stronger color by boiling the water down to smaller quantity. Use part of this onion water to combine with red beet juice to make orange. Among the other natural dyes used to color eggs yellow are grains, hay, saffron, crocuses and daffodils.

RED: Cook 3 or 4 large beets with their skins on, in 2 cups water. After you drain the water, the beets can be used to eat. Simply slip off the skins and add your seasonings. Carrots, red cabbage, radishes and crushed red clay are used in various parts of the world to produce shades of red.

GREEN: Just about any greens can be cooked (1 lb. to 1½ cups water) to get various shades of green. For example young grass, escarole, sage, spinach, broccoli.

BLUE: Blueberries make the best blue. They can be used even out of season, by buying a box of frozen blueberries, and draining the juice off the berries. It is such a strong color that you can add water if necessary without much loss of color. Purple anemones are used in France and other countries. With this information, you might want to experiment with other vegetables — squashes, pumpkin etc. In season, you can gather marigold flower heads. You'll need a dozen flower heads simmered for an hour in 2 cups of water to make a good color.

BROWN: Plums, red onions, coffee, bark of tree, and old walnut shells, are boiled to produce a wide range of browns.

Polish the dyed eggs with a few drops of vegetable oil on a cloth.

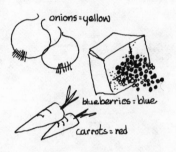

onions = yellow

blueberries = blue

carrots = red

COMMERCIAL DYES

Vegetable dyes made for coloring eggs are available in the baking section of any food market all year, and in five-and-ten-cent stores around Easter time. Choose tiny bottles of concentrated liquid or tablets and follow the directions given by the manufacturer.

DYEING THE YARN

A more interesting type of staining is achieved by wrapping bright-colored yarns around the shell, then boiling the whole egg in water for 20 minutes. The different colors and textures of the yarns leave patterns on the shell when the yarn is removed after the eggs cool.

Plate 21. *If you're lucky enough to have one, an antique stand such as was used in grandmother's day could hold eggs while they are being dyed or decorated. There's a handpainted egg on the scale at the right.*

DYEING WITH LEAVES

A method of dyeing which combines natural and manmade materials is very effective. Place a leaf or two, such as the new leaves on the tips of branches, around the eggshell to make an interesting silhouette. Tie the leaf in place by wrapping the eggs in a cloth (cheesecloth, muslin, or any colorfast scrap from your fabric bag). Soak wrapped egg for five hours in commercial vegetable coloring, prepared as directed on the package. Remove egg from dye bath, take off the cloth and foliage, and the outline of the leaf on the shell will be unique.

DYEING BEADS

If you want to change the tints of white pearls, you can do so successfully using Rit (but some of the cheaper imports seem to resist dyes). For a pale tint of any desired color, dip white pearls into a solution of 1 teaspoon dye to 1 cup of hot water. For a deeper tone, keep adding dye, up to about 2 teaspoons. Rinse just as manufacturer directs for fabric and let dry.

EMBOSSING WITH WAX

Embossing adds another dimension to egg design. Pure beeswax makes the raised areas. You will need:
Chicken eggs, 1 dozen
commercial egg coloring, your color choice
pure beeswax (in flat sheets or thick squares)
Eastman 910 adhesive.

103

Here's how you do it:
Step One. Empty the eggs by blowing out the contents (see Chapter 8)

Step Two. Dye the eggs

Step Three. Flatten the beeswax, which is pliable, to a thinner layer, depending upon how high a raised area you would like I prefer 3/16-inch thick.

Step Four. Cut squares and strips of the wax with a large scissors or an X-acto knife.

Step Five. There are two ways to attach your designs to the colored eggshell. One way is to melt a little of the beeswax in a small tin can set in boiling water and use the melted wax as if it were glue. Another is to put a drop of the Eastman Kodak 910 on the eggshell to hold on the design. The wax may be painted with Testors paint or left its natural color.

Step Six. While the wax is fairly soft, you can press "jewels," stones, tiny shells, beads, seeds or other natural materials into the wax.

Step Seven. Insead of plain wax, glue a cutout picture to a wax base and glue them both to the egg.

ETCHING

Etching can be as simple or as intricate as you wish. Even the plainest design, however, will be interesting because of the texture you create and the delicacy of the lines. You'll get greater satisfaction from a design you create yourself, rather than copy. But you can also choose to adapt one from the rich folk art available, for example in Pennsylvania Dutch designs. You can etch the whole egg, or just a portion of it (for instance the door, if you are using a large egg that is to become a jewel box or similar show piece).

You will need a simple scratch board knife or a sharp needle for etching. Work directly on the plain eggshell for a subtle design, or get a bolder effect by painting the egg first and then etching the lines with acid.

Goose, duck or chicken eggs should be etched with the contents inside to support the shell and give it the extra strength needed to withstand the pressure of the tool. When you have finished etching, the contents can be blown out or removed after you cut a door or lid.

Ostrich, rhea or emu eggs are durable enough to be etched empty. Since these eggs come from other countries, they will be shipped empty to comply with public health regulations.

The etched ostrich egg is beautiful. It is a creamy white and the design will usually be a purer white.

Etching on the dark green of the emu egg produces a lovely soft green color for contrast.

SCRATCH METHOD

Step One. Always work on a clean egg.

Step Two. Make your design on paper before you transfer it to the egg. This will allow you to change anything you don't like at this time.

Step Three. Transfer the design to the eggshell with a pencil, either freehand, or by tracing. Simple designs are best.

Step Four. Using your scratch board knife, apply enough pressure to your draw lines to cut your design into the surface of the shell.

Step Five. Dip egg in commercial dye to color. Etched lines will take more dye and appear darker.

Step Six. Depth can be added to the design on the ostrich egg by soaking it in the water and coffee grounds from leftover coffee, after etching. The more coffee grounds you use, the deeper the brown. Only the etched areas will take the stain, making an interesting contrast.

ACID METHOD

Step One. Paint the entire egg with black India ink. Let dry for 10 minutes.

Step Two. Buy a two-ounce bottle of a 3% solution of hydrochloric acid at the drug store. Dip your scratch into the bottle and sketch your design on the egg freehand. The acid will remove the color. Pat dry with a soft cloth to remove any excess acid. *Do not get it on your skin and don't let the children get at it!* It can cause a burn. Protect your hands with rubber gloves. If you should get hydrochloric acid on your skin, immediately wash thoroughly with clear water.

Step Three. For children, let them scratch their design with sauerkraut juice. It will not work as well as the acid, but it is safe.

GILDING (GOLD LEAFING)

This truly beautiful finish can be applied in several ways, depending upon whether you buy the liquid, paste or leaf paper. All are found in art, paint or hobby stores. For an antiqued effect, try a coat of paint over the egg, then a layer of gold leaf.

Leaf is applied to blown eggs, or eggs with openings. You can use an egg rack as described in chapter I, or gild the door or lid, let it dry, then use that as your handle while finishing the egg.

LIQUID LEAF is the easiest to apply. You simply paint it on with a brush.

PASTE WAX LEAF must be rubbed on with your fingers or a soft cloth. Since it is a wax, it requires buffing, and sometimes must be followed by a second application of gold and additional buffing.

METAL LEAF is recommended for beginners, rather than the more expensive real gold leaf. Its only disadvantage is that it will tarnish unless you use a decoupage sealer after you've applied it. Glue the leaf paper carefully to the eggshell and tap gently with a soft cloth or brush to transfer it to the eggshell. Be careful not to tear the paper in this process.

REAL GOLD LEAF comes in 3-inch x 3-inch squares in a limited number of shades. The sheets have been pounded so unbelievably thin that the slightest breeze can crumble it. It comes with a protective sheet above and under it. Peel off only one of these layers, leaving the bottom protected. Glue the leaf side to the eggshell and gently rub the surface of the protective paper with a swab of cotton to secure the leaf to the egg. Secure any loose edges by gently blowing on them. Repeat the process until the desired surface is covered.

LACQUER FINISHES

Lacquers are beautiful on the jewel box eggs, and the finished product often looks like copper enamel. Lacquer should be flowed on generously, always brushing in only one direction to avoid air-bubbles. I paint the egg under high intensity light; the heat from the bulb sets up the lacquer almost immediately. Additional coats of lacquer may be applied to obtain the desired effects, but be sure to allow the egg to dry completely between applications of lacquer.

    Although it takes practice to do a lacquer finish in many layers, it's a magnificent finish, and it's in the Fabergé tradition.

Plate 22. *Liquid leaf can also be brushed on inside the egg, as here, in this open view of the scallop cut goose egg shown in Chapter 3. Lining an egg like this can be quite a challenge. After ten tries, I purchased white kid, the kind used for gloves, and contoured it to the inside. It was smashing! However, working with leather is an ordeal and time-consuming, so I now use the liquid leaf. On the very bottom of the shell, I place my weights and a platform, with a small puff of white silk to hold the jewelry.*

I have tried many kinds of lacquers, but Testors model airplane lacquer works best for me and it comes in many colors. Another Testors lacquer, called metal flake, gives a finish with an enameled look. It, too, comes in a wide range of colors. Whatever lacquer you use, *it must be fresh*. Fresh lacquer stirs easily. Old lacquer is hard on the bottom and difficult to stir. (At one time I used an Oriental lacquer but abandoned it when I found it was difficult to obtain and was not always fresh.)

APPLYING THE LACQUER

Step One. Always apply lacquer either vertically or horizontally, but don't change direction; the brush strokes should be applied parallel to each other. Brush it on (remember, I use a size six inexpensive camel hair brush, but I pull out any loose hairs).

Step Two. Do not rush the drying process or you will have random buildup of lacquer in spots. Allow at least three hours between coats.

Step Three. Continue the lacquering and drying process until you have up to a total of eight coats. This will produce a very high gloss and a three-dimensional effect. If you are satisfied with the result, you might stop at three or four coats.

Step Four. After the final coat has been applied, dry the egg for twenty-four hours.

Step Five. Now you are ready for the splendor and the fun of applying trimmings.

Plate 23. Lacquering the door under high intensity light, I brush in one direction. You can see why I suggest using a color on the teardrop door. It emphasizes the graceful cut and adds elegance. Even a door needs several coats of paint, and be sure to allow proper drying between coats. Overnight is safest. Also, do not permit paint to build up on the hinge; remove splotches immediately if they occur.

Step One. Lacquer is not easy for everyone to apply. Not only does it tend to run, but it builds up in some areas, especially around the cut edge. To avoid this, stir lacquer very carefully before you begin, and make sure you get *fresh* lacquer.

Step Two. Generally, using a thinner reduces the luster of the finish and may cause runs. However, if runs or lacquer build-up have already occurred, use thinner on the problem area only, and hope for the best. Dip a clean brush in the thinner and spot-touch the area in question very sparingly. Let this area dry thoroughly (at least ½ hour) before adding more lacquer. When you apply the next coat, paint the entire egg.

Step Three. Avoid sanding since it produces unwanted texture.

Step Four. If something goes seriously wrong, I recommend that you discard the egg and start a new one. Don't waste your efforts on an egg with a large flaw. Sometimes you can cover a small mistake with trim, but when you have to add so much trim that you lose the basic design, you end up with an over-decorated egg.

MARBLEIZING

I had a marvelous time developing marbleizing, which creates remarkably different patterns on the shell. It is a dramatic finish, but hard to trim because marbleizing produces lots of pattern for its small area. On the other hand, you probably won't *want* to trim this attractively decorated shell.

I prefer using a *blown* egg because, when you dip an egg with a door, both the *inside* and *outside* become marbleized. Marbleizing is a dramatic finish but it is harder to trim because marbleizing produces a lot of pattern for the small area.

I use at least two colors, but the following directions apply no matter how many colors you use. This is best for any whole, blown eggs.

Step One. You'll need a bowl that is at least twice the diameter and depth of the egg you will be marbleizing — to give you plenty of room to swish the egg around. The bowl will be discarded so it is practical to use a plastic one.

Step Two. Fill a bowl three-quarters full with tap water at room temperature.

Step Three. Empty two or more one-ounce bottles of Testors paint into the water and stir gently with a stick. Each color will remain intact; this paint will not form a homogenous mixture. I especially like blue and green, but black and brown (which gives a tortoise effect) or red and metallic gold are very attractive. Use any combination that simulates marble, or create fantasy effects.

Step Four. Carefully dip the egg into the mixture, turning the egg as you dip. You can use a bought wire egg holder, a hibachi stick, or improvise by poking a wire (the kind used for beading) through the holes in the egg and looping the end of the wire.

Step Five. Remove quickly and *do not re-dip*.

Step Six. Allow to dry (about 20 minutes).

Step Seven. Stir the mixture each time before dipping.

There might be times that you *do* want to dip a hinged egg (for example, if you are planning a jewel box with a marbleized exterior and fabric lining the interior, so it won't matter what finish is inside). Here's how to proceed: Hold the cut section while you dip the rest. Dry it face down with the door open. When dry (in about 20 minutes), you can hold onto the marbleized side, and then dip the door.

Plate 24. The tiny little quail egg on the left is the smallest I work with. Its entire inside has been pearlized, and the opening edged in gold braid. Then a row of 2mm pearls, and another row of gold braid, were added. The base is a tiny plastic cap that can also be bought in a gold finish. The delightful miniature figures are a pair of Irish dancers, whose upraised hands create an oval that repeats the outside form.

Another unusual egg—this time an araucana chicken egg from South America—(right) is marbleized as described on page 111. As you can see, the swirls produce a lot of design and texture, so any additional trim must be restrained. The colors are blue-greens so I used just one single row of gold cord around the cut edges. It is, of course, a jewel case. On the very top, I added three tiny gold leaves and one small pearl. The base too, is very simple and also very inexpensive.

PAINTS AND PAINTING

You may want to spray-paint or brush-paint your eggs, but the lacquer finish is so much more effective that I urge you to use it, if it's a really elegant enameled finish you're trying to achieve; see page 107 for details of lacquers and lacquering.

Many people have a propensity for leaving brushes in the paint after use, rendering costly brushes worthless. I find the inexpensive camel hair brushes of the ten to fifteen cent variety work just as well. All hobby shops carry them and I use size six; it holds more paint yet handles well. Before you use an inexpensive brush, try to remove any loose hairs, since its worst characteristic is that it frequently sheds. Merely by tugging at the hairs on the end of the brush, you'll remove stray bristles. It takes only one hair embedded in the paint on the eggshell to ruin the finish.

PEARLIZING

The pearlizing finish can be achieved with either one of two materials: pearlized nail polish, or mother-of-pearl chips. With the former method apply six coats of the frosted fingernail polish (which is actually a lacquer) allowing four hours drying time between coats.

The mother-of-pearl chips come in small packets. Each packet will cover 3 medium-size goose eggs completely. Applying it requires a great deal of time; it is applied as follows:

Step One. Cover a small area of the eggshell with Elmer's glue.

Step Two. Carefully place the mother-of-pearl, piece by piece, in the glue-covered spot.

Step Three. Repeat the process in small areas until the egg is completely covered with chips. Doing only a small section at a time, the glue remains moist until each chip is properly placed.

Step Four. Allow the egg to dry at least eight hours.

Step Five. Gently paint a decoupage sealer over the mother-of-pearl. This will seal the finish and add luster.

PRESSED FLOWER DECORATIONS

Long-lasting materials from the garden or wayside make enchanting appliqués for eggs that appeal to ecological-minded craftsmen. You can use seed pods, grasses, flowers, leaves, and grains, but they must be treated and dried, not only to assure their longevity once they are applied to the egg, but also because living fresh garden materials have natural succulence, which does not accept glues well. Select material when it is in bloom and dry it to insure year-round supply. Always dry more than you need to allow for spoilage. If you can label the plants now, do so. It's amazing how the change in the form and color from natural to dried state causes memory lapses and as a result you may forget what you are using.

WHAT TO DRY: There is virtually no limit to the type of material you can dry and press for your egg designs. Select small-scaled materials that fit the egg. For example, the compound clusters of rhododendron blossom, panicles from the stalk of oats or catalpa, and racemes from the lily of the valley can produce a tremendous amount of material. Pick the flowers when they are fresh, and pick only the best specimens.

HOW TO DRY: Press plant materials (butterflies too) between sheets of paper toweling placed in a magazine and weighted down with books, bricks, etc. Check the paper toweling once or twice as it absorbs moisture. Change papers if they are damp as the plants may mildew.

WHAT ABOUT COLOR: Some flower lovers insist that flowers be used naturally, but dried plant materials are often painted or sprayed even by garden-club members and flower-show exhibitors (unless the rules of the show prohibit doing so). You can paint or spray your dried plants in a wide choice of colors to compliment room colors, or use commercial sprays or rub with Treasure Gold. You can gild the plant material to match the base.

SEED PODS: Seeds are often used in decoration. Cut open the pods when they are not yet ripe and place the seeds on blotting paper to dry naturally. Be sure the room is dry; a basement area near the furnace would be fine.

BASES FOR NATURAL PLANTS: A tree trunk holder, animal forms or driftwood and plant-decorated eggs have a natural affinity for each other.

Small pieces of weathered wood, including tree roots and small sections of logs, are easy to buy or to find and fashion into bases yourself. Sterilize any piece of wood before you use it, if insect life could be present, by giving it a bath in boiling water. Then test it with a pick to be sure it has not rotted at crucial spots. Remove any decay and sand, break or saw away whatever you must to provide a cavity, and to be sure that the wood can rest on a flat surface.

HERE ARE SOME OF THE POSSIBLE FINISHES:

116   You can paint the driftwood with any commercial paint; dip it into Clorox to bleach it, shine it up with shoe polish, or glaze, gild or lacquer it using the same materials used for eggs, following the manufacturer's directions for wood.

METHOD FOR PRESSED FLOWER APPLIQUE

Step One. Handle flowers as little as possible once they are dried. Arrange your design on paper before transferring it, petal by petal and leaf by leaf to the glue-area on the egg. It can be arranged in a natural or an abstract design. Use tweezers to transfer the plant material to the egg, and press it firmly against the glue. Do not try to move it around once applied, as it is very fragile. Carefully clean away any excess glue using a wet cue tip (water is the solvent for Elmer's glue). You can also use Eastman 910 which has its own bonding solvent. Work carefully so you don't displace anything. Finish by spraying with several coats of fixative. The dried plant materials are a little more trouble than other appliqués, but the effect is charming.

Step Two. Add any embellishments like braids, embroidery threads or yarns for a finishing touch.

Step Three. For tree ornaments, attach a purchased hook through the hole made when blowing out the contents, (see Making Hangers for Decorated Eggs in Chapter 2).

PORCELAIN FINISH

You can use the much admired porcelain finish on a blown egg or one with a door. In the latter case, be sure to cut and hinge it before applying the finish. Here's how to achieve a perfect finish:

Step One. Dye the egg with vegetable dye in any color, keeping in mind that the finished egg will look lighter.

Step Two. Apply seven or eight coats (one at a time), of Elmer's white glue, with an inexpensive brush. Allow each coat to dry thoroughly before covering with the next coat. Use an egg rack to dry.

Step Three. After all the layers of glue have been applied (each time *brushing* it on), spray the egg with a high-gloss clear lacquer.

Step Four. You might find it easier to brush the lacquer on, rather than spray it. Either way, allow it to dry between each coat for at least four hours. Use at least four coats of the lacquer. When finished, you will have built up many coats that will not only add depth to the egg but give a protective coating as well.

Step Five. Allow the egg to dry on an egg rack. (Directions for making it are in Chapter 2) This is not an overnight procedure. To thoroughly dry, set aside for at least thirty-six hours.

PYSANKY

This charming folk art, named for the Ukrainian word *pysaty*, meaning *to write,* is a cousin to batik. It was practiced under different names in the rural areas of Poland, Rumania, Moravia, Greece, and Yugoslavia. It is still a cherished craft in parts of the United States where immigrants from those European countries settled. Eggs so decorated were given as gifts and ornaments, not as food.

In some countries, whole raw chicken eggs were used, in others, the eggs were hard-boiled first, but in either case (no doubt because of the association of eggs with enduring life) the peasants believed that eggs decorated for Easter would never get rotten.

If your own faith is weaker, you might prefer to blow out the eggs before you ornament them.

Directions follow for a five-color egg design, which takes time and patience. Beginners might want to work with just two colors, or even one color in several shades, for practice. Dyes can be vegetable dyes or fabric dyes.

Step One. Pysanky is a high form of doodling and you design-as-you-go. You will need a special stylus called a kistka, (in olden days, you might have used a thorn) which allows a very fine stream of wax to flow. With the kistka, you can doodle in wax as if you were using a pen. If you want a very symmetrical design, it is a good idea to divide your egg into four equal parts with two rubber bands. For a more complex symmetrical design, divide each of the four parts into six more sections.

The motif in each of the six sections, will be repeated exactly on all the other like sections. You then make a design on one quarter of the egg and repeat it on each of the other three quarters. You can design freeform or geometrically, but if you were Ukrainian, your designs would be traditional, and would indicate the region from which you come.

Step Two. Mix your dyes according to the directions on the package. Melt the beeswax in a can set in hot water.

Step Three. If you cannot work freehand, mark your design with *very* light lines, using a hard pencil. If lines are dark, dye will not cover them.

Step Four. Using the kistka (a special egg-decorating stylus), trace over the first color in your design (the lightest). In this case, it will be white. Whatever is covered with wax will remain white.

119

Step Five. Now with the next palest color, yellow, immerse the egg in dye, let stand up to half an hour, remove and allow to dry.

Step Six. Dipping your kistka in wax, cover any part of the design that is to remain yellow. Allow to dry.

Step Seven. If you want any green areas, apply blue dye at this stage, using a brush over those yellow areas that you would like to be green.

Step Eight. Dip egg in orange dye. Allow to dry.

Step Nine. With wax, cover any part you wish to remain orange.

Step Ten. Dip in red (or whatever your own darkest color is). Allow to dry.

Step Eleven. Do not scratch off the wax, you will mar the design. Just dip the egg into hot (not boiling) water for a few seconds.

Ukrainian egg designs played a large part in their religious life, and some of the motifs and the meanings are shown below:

Triangle — air, fire, water or the Holy Trinity

8-Pointed Star — ancient sun-god

sun — good fortune

chicken or rooster — fulfillment of wishes

deer — wealth, prosperity

fir tree — eternal youth, health

fish — ancient symbol of Christ

flower — love, charity

endless line — eternity

triangle

8 pointed star

sun

fir tree

fish

120

flower

endless line

SUMMARY OF STEPS IN DECORATING THE SHELL

Step One. Prepare your egg. You can start with appliqué, which is quite simple, and follow the step-by-step methods, but eventually I hope you will attempt to do the lacquers. (Lacquered eggs are the real reason for my writing this book!)

Step Two. When the shell is decorated and dried, select a non-tarnishable trim. Inexpensive trims waste both your talent and your time as they will undermine the total effect. Same with the stones — good ones cost but a few pennies more than the cheapest imports. The ones I like best are the Austrian stones, because they have greater color density and brilliance than any of the others.

Step Three. Mount your trimmed egg on a base consistent with the total look you want to achieve. Bases created specifically for eggs are available on the current market in many designs and finishes. (see Chapter 7).

6

Jewel Boxes

*"Like stones of worth they thinly placed are, or
captain jewels in the carcanet."*
— Shakespeare Sonnet

THIS IS THE NAME GIVEN TO ANY EGG WHICH HAS A HINGED LID
and fabric lining. It is one of the most popular styles in decorated eggs, and there is almost no limit to the cuts and finishes
you can use in making them. I always give jewel boxes a lacquer
finish in one of the exciting colors which Fabergé might have
used — deep reds, royal blues and lustrous greens.

Each egg should be developed with a theme in mind, and
the particular cut and trim selected to carry out that theme. The
egg designed without proper proportion or with unrelated colors
is a disaster.

The jewel box is best made from the goose egg which has
the strong shell needed for the cutting and handling it will receive. Its size and shape makes it readily adaptable to many
designs. Cut the lid as described in Chapter 3, and empty it.

WEIGHTING THE JEWEL BOX

An empty eggshell is so very lightweight that when placed
on a high stand it becomes unsteady and may tip over and break.

(If the jewel box is to be mounted on an extremely heavy base, weighting may not be necessary. It's necessary only for jewel boxes, not other kinds of eggs.) Added weight in the bottom half of the egg will counteract this tendency and will also make the box more durable. You will need bb's or fishing line weights (both found at sporting good stores). The bb's come in 4 oz. boxes.

Step One. Fill the bottom of the egg with weights. Use about 1 oz. of weight for each large goose egg, and proportionately less for smaller eggs.

Step Two. Cover the weights completely by spreading Elmer's glue all around them.

Step Three. Stir out airpockets with a small stick and make sure there are no little loose bb's left to rattle around.

Step Four. Cover the weights with a platform cut from a piece of card stock. Trace the diameter of the cut half of the egg on the card, then trim down the circle until it fits snugly over the weights. If the glue holding the bb's has dried, spread another layer of glue on the bottom of the platform before pressing it down to conceal the weights.

When weighting an egg that is to have a drawer, use fewer bb's so that you can open and close the drawer easily.

DRAPED OR PUFFY LINING FOR THE JEWEL BOX

CHOOSING FABRICS

The fabric plays an important role in lining; if too sheer, for example, it will not drape gracefully. It might have body as well as a soft texture, and a lustrous sheen for highlights. A soft silk taffeta best fulfills all these requirements. I do not recommend brocades. They are usually very stiff and, unless the pattern is very small, they look too heavy and overpower the design of the egg. (I am referring here only to fabric for a draped lining because I do use brocade to make flat, one-dimensional linings for doors and egg interiors; see plate 7.)

White or soft pastel colors are best. Dark browns and black make the egg heavy and funereal-looking. Do not use cotton in the bottom of the jewel box to puff up the fabric; the fabric itself will drape more naturally without it.

LINING METHOD:

When adding the lining, always start with the bottom section of the egg first. It is a simple operation and can be done by following these directions:

Step One. I am giving cutting directions for a specific egg; a goose egg, 4 inches long. The diameter opening was 2½ inches. For this egg, I cut a rectangular piece of fabric 8 inches long and 5 inches wide.

Step Two. Make parallel cuts one inch long and one inch apart along the bottom of the fabric to help it contour to the inside of the shell.

Step Three. Cut the points off the upper corners of the fabric.

Step Four. Fold over one end on itself, hem fashion, then glue the inside of this flap with Sobo glue to make a neat edge. You now have a sleeve.

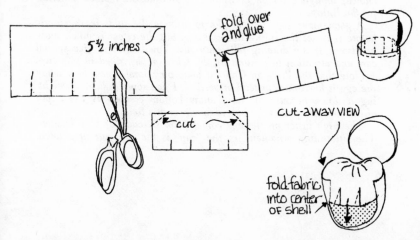

5½ inches

fold over and glue

cut

CUT-aWaV VIEW

fold fabric into center of shell

Step Five. Glue the bottom edge of the sleeve to the rim of the bottom half of the shell.

Step Six. Drop a small amount of glue through the center of the sleeve, into the bottom of the shell.

Step Seven. Gather the edges and fold the outside of the sleeve into the center of the egg until the end touches the glue. The excess fabric will drape itself with just a little help from your fingertips.

Step Eight. Using the same method, with a smaller width of fabric, line the top part of the egg.

Step Nine. This method can be used for all linings with minor variations dictated by the size and shape of the particular egg. Additional small cuts in the fabric may be necessary to achieve a better fit for the pointed cuts, but, with any modification, you must use extra glue to insure smoothness of the lining.

Plate 25. (Opposite)   A draped lining must be luxurious and full, so remember to allow plenty of fabric when you cut. It's a fairly easy step in egg crafting, but only if you follow the text carefully, and work meticulously. You should get a pleasing effect, even the first time you drape the lining. White silk taffeta is my usual fabric choice, though I do on occasion use brocades and other materials for flat linings.

A good many egg crafters like to arrange the folds in the fabric before they set the lining into the egg, but the effect is much more handsome if the draping falls naturally. You'll have to give special care and attention to contouring the fabric as described in step two.

126   *Note that the Prussian Cap cut takes on a totally new look when the egg is horizontal instead of vertical. I had some difficulty weighting it down because of the shallow bottom created by the depth of the cut but I pasted the bb's in one layer at a time.*

The high luster on the egg comes from six coats of blue lacquer. The interesting ornament on the "cap" is the top part of a latch.

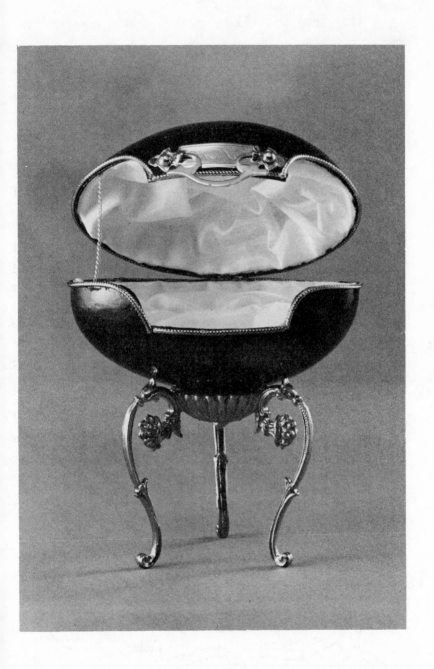

The egg with a drawer is very unusual. Again I stress precision, for the drawer must open freely and must fit back into its original position in the egg.

It is not possible to put a drawer in all types of eggs. Many eggs are much too fragile to withstand the handling involved. The goose egg is the best of the domestic egg for this purpose. But ostrich, emu, and rhea eggs are also excellent because of their heavy shells.

CUTTING AND FITTING THE DRAWER. To start the basic drawer, cut a rectangular piece of shell below the center of the egg. I use the box made for the small wooden matches for the actual drawer. Place the narrow end of the match box in the proper position against the egg and trace all around it with a pencil. Cut the opening just a shade larger so box will slide. The rectangular piece cut from the egg will convex because of the shape of the egg. Using Elmer's glue, secure this convex rectangular piece of shell to the front of the matchbox.

There will be a space between the eggshell and the matchbox, both top and bottom. This can be covered with a light piece of paper cut to fit the area as illustrated. When the jewel box is eventually painted this paper can also be painted, giving the drawer a more finished appearance.

128

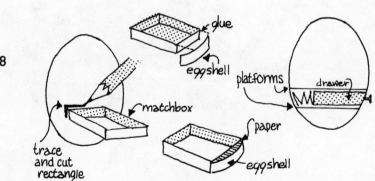

Since the drawer must slide back into the egg without any mechanical devices or guides, it is necessary to build a platform below the drawer. This can be constructed from an oval piece of heavy card stock cut to fit the egg cavity just below the location of the drawer. Dab glue lightly around the circumference of the card and turn it over when placing it inside the egg. After inserting the drawer, construct another platform in the same fashion above the drawer; it will then glide in and out between the two platforms without binding.

Usually the back of the matchbox will not reach the opposite side of the shell, but the drawer will hang better within the egg if some contact is made between the box and the shell. This can be done with a small piece of accordion-folded paper which, when glued to the back of the drawer, will function as a spring-like bumper against the shell.

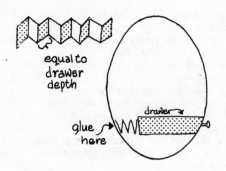

equal to
drawer
depth

glue
here

drawer

TO MAKE A PAPER BUMPER FOR DRAWER

I save the paper from old greeting cards for drawer bumpers, since a firm and flexible good-quality paper is needed. Cut a long rectangle almost as wide as your matchbox and longer than you think you will need (at least 8 inches). Fold the strip accordion-style, making each section as deep as the depth of the matchbox drawer. Now you will have to experiment. Try your bumper out by attaching it to the back of the drawer. Snip off the folds from the other end, one-by-one until you have the proper amount of "accordion" to fill in the space behind the drawer. Then glue it to the inside of the egg directly opposite the back of the drawer. A matching silk lining may be added to the inside of the drawer. You can use a small plastic, or even metal box; however they are much more difficult to work because they are hard to glue and hard to trim.

Plate 26. Looking rather like a bombe chest, this super-size goose egg (double yolk) is made with a single door plus a drawer—not an easy combination but the result enchants all who see it. I even added two filigree windows in the back.

The finish is a beautiful jade green metal flake which required just four coats of lacquer, and after 24 hours of drying it was ready for trimming. I edged the complete opening and drawer with gold cord. Then I used Tiffany-type pearls and another edging of gold cord. I covered the tiny holes on the hinge with flat-sided gold dots. This gives the illusion that the hinge is bolted on (although it is glued only). On the very top I used a gold filigree, topped with a gold filigree ball. I used the same gold filigree ball in a smaller size for the drawer pull.

All jewel boxes need a chain to take the stress off the hinge when the lid is open, and to keep the top from flopping all the way open. The chain holds the lid in an attractive half-open position.

Step One. Place the chain enough forward from the hinge so that it will drop neatly inside the jewel box when the top is closed. If placed too close to the hinge, it will drop outside, instead.

Step Two. Choose a fine jewelry-type chain because it comes in many pretty designs, will not tarnish and is not expensive. I always match silver-trimmed eggs with a silver chain, and gold with gold.

Step Three. Glue a 2½ inch length of chain against the inside of the bottom half of the egg with Eastman 910 adhesive.

Step Four. Add the lining to the bottom (directions follow). When it is glued in place (with Sobo glue), it will doubly secure the chain.

Step Five. Let the chain and the bottom part of the lined jewel box dry completely before starting the top part.

Plate 27. (Opposite) *This Queen Anne cut jewel box is a favorite of mine. It took a painstaking eight coats of lime gold metal flake paint to get that beautiful finish. The egg is a medium-size goose egg. I edged the entire rim of the bottom and the lid with gold roping. The top, only, was trimmed with Tiffany-style pearls and another row of gold roping. By keeping the trimming quite simple, I was able to use the graceful sea horse base without detracting from the overall effect. I used a white lining, as I almost always do, because there is no conflict between it and any other color in the design. The decoration on the point is a blue-green finding that was part of a dangle earring. I watch constantly for earrings that might be suitable to use on the front of jewel boxes. This egg is in the collection of Mrs. Robert Beale of Rochester, New York and was purchased at the Memorial Art Gallery.*

Step Six. When dry, line the top of the box, gluing it in with Sobo glue and when the lining is in position, tease the fabric back sufficiently to stuff the chain under it in the proper position. The add a little more Eastman 910 adhesive to the eggshell, bonding shell and chain together. Reglue the lining with Sobo glue, over the chain.

FINISHING THE JEWEL BOX

If all the steps have been followed meticulously the egg design is now almost completed. Inspect it carefully looking for tiny Elmer's glue spots and remove them with a bit of cotton dipped in water. Buff with a clean cloth to remove any fingerprints.

The finish of the paint or lacquer should serve as the final coat. An unpainted egg in its natural shell can be finished with decoupage sealer. Brush it on gently at the very end, rather than sealing it early, for the trims do not adhere to the shell after the sealer has been applied.

Precision is most important. If you're going to feel rushed, put the jewel box egg aside and work on another egg. This kind of cut egg requires not only dexterity, but emotional discipline and patience as well.

After building the egg with one drawer, you may find it a challenge to try the egg with two drawers. Use a long, fat egg in order to have room for all the required platforms. Follow the directions for one drawer, simply allowing a larger opening. The double drawer develops the look of the bombé chest and

lends itself to decoration of decoupage.

7

Finishing Touches: Linings, Insets, Trims And Bases

"But there is something beyond — a higher point, a subtle and unmistakable touch of love and pride beyond mere skill; almost an inspiration which gives to all work that finish which is almost art — which is art."
— Joseph Conrad, *The Mirror of the Sea*

EGG DECORATING IS THE HOBBY OF EXTREMES. AFTER YOU HAVE bought a few basic tools, you can have much pleasure and satisfaction without spending more than a few pennies for eggs and decorations. Braids and ribbons from Christmas packages, wood bases that you make yourself, prints cut from cards are yours for the salvaging.

On the other hand, you can spend the equivalent of a king's ransom on real jewels, handmade edgings, rare figurines, antique bases and every kind of luxurious and elegant material found in nature or made by man to ornament and individualize your egg.

Somewhere in between these two extremes, you'll find a whole range of possibilities. For edging and finishing, there are cords of all sorts in two-tones and metallics, as well as rickrack, soutache, woven tapes, twine, wool yarns, crochet threads and thin macrame cords. One caution, even though I'm repeating myself, always buy non-tarnishing materials because the other kind isn't worth the time you'll put into your project.

For little frills on egg cradles and such, you'll want lace and lace paper, ruching, netting, and ruffles.

As inlays and overlays there are cameos, seashells, buttons, tassels, pompons, mother-of-pearl, pearls and beads which come prestrung, and flat-back rhinestones that look like rubies, sapphires and other precious stones.

For linings, there are fabrics in abundance, mother-of-pearl and rows of pearls and braids.

For decoupaging the interior of an egg, you'll use fancy metallic papers, pictures from magazines, wallpaper scraps or prints, even oddments left from bigger decoupaging projects.

So I'm not going to be didactic about what to buy, and not to buy, for your finishing egg decorating venture, except to say that:

a) The three basic trims that I would twist myself into knots to acquire are Wrights Chinese braid, gold cord and gold bullion.

b) Any material that you want can be bought by mail if you cannot buy it locally.

c) Remember to use Elmer's glue to apply lightweight cords and trims, Sobo glue to glue fabric linings into jewel box eggs, and Eastman 910 for hinges, chains and latches; to attach jewels and miniatures to the egg; and to attach heavy braids to large heavy eggs.

136

before lining...
glue
chain
here

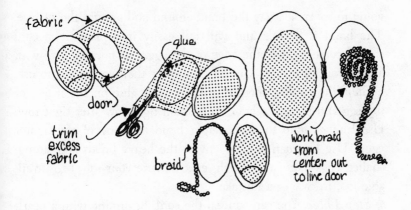

fabric

glue

door

trim
excess
fabric

braid

work braid
from
center out
to line door

LINING INTERIORS WITH FABRIC

I sometimes use a lining of fabric inside. Here's how it works:

Step One. Lay the egg down on the fabric of your choice and cut a square of fabric larger than the door. Spread a thin film of Sobo glue all around the inside of the door to be lined and then lay the square of fabric on the door. Press gently but firmly down on the fabric, working from the center out, to remove all air bubbles and make the lining as flat and wrinkleproof as is humanly possible.

Step Two. Trim off the edges of the fabric as close to the egg as possible. Paste cord around the edges of the fabric for a finished look. Then let the whole thing dry overnight.

BRAID LINING

You'll note that many of my eggs are lined with row after row of braiding. The same procedure applies to adding rows of cord inside and outside the door. Here's how I do it:

137

Step One. Before you get down to the nitty gritty of doing it, take the braid and, starting in the middle of the space you're going to cover, just lay the braid around and around the surface. The braid is flexible and will fall easily into place. The cord should come right to the edge of the egg, but not interfere with any of your openings. Cut off a bit more than you expect to use.

Step Two. Now for the real job. Put glue on the inside of the egg and place the braid in position tight row after tight row. Use Elmer's glue for lightweight braid and any of the lighter eggs. Use Eastman 910 for any of the heavy braids and strong-shelled eggs like emu, ostrich, etc. Be sure your solvent is available too, in case of a mistake.

Step Three. You can conceal the cord, beginning with a pearl, small painted ceramic etc., the braid ending can be concealed if necessary, with another row of contrasting braid.

HOW TO APPLY THE TRIMMINGS

Trimmings are not only ornamental, they are also functional since they help strengthen the cut egg and conceal the joinings and edges of doors. As far as I can recall, every cut egg I have ever designed has been edged with some kind of trimming. Sometimes I use just one narrow border of fine cord, or I alternate cords, stones, braids etc. in separate rows. Or I'm just as likely to use a continuous row of the same cord, braid or string of jewels. It's fun to do many different styles of trimmings — inside, outside or all around the egg. Whatever your choice of ornament, here's the basic procedure for adding the trimmings:

138   *Step One.* Cut off the necessary amount of cord, trim, or braid, adding a little extra for safety. If it is cut off first, the trimming is less likely to twist and curl as you paste it. Later, with experience, you might wish to work from the roll, as I do.

Step Two. You must always start applying the trim at the edge of the egg, beginning at one side of the hinge and ending on the other and invariably, working from the cut edge into the center.

Step Three. Squeeze a thin line of Elmer's glue right from the container onto the egg, all around the edge where the first row of trimming is to go. Push each row next to the other as you paste down the trim, to make a tight fit.

Step Four. If braid seems to fray at the cut end (not a typical problem — it rarely does if you use the right kind) put a dab of decoupage sealer on the ends (or a dab of glue underneath the ends) to hold them. Push all rows of braids and trims closely together so each row fits tightly — but not so tightly that the material gaps.

Caution: Do not use prepasted trims or braids; they often fall off the egg. If you've bought them, just apply with glue and ignore the prepasting.

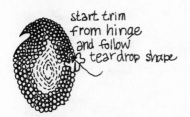

start trim from hinge and follow teardrop shape

trim follows all the various contours of intricate cuts

HOW TO APPLY PRESTRUNG PEARLS AND JEWELS

I do not use knotted beads, preferring the smooth line of closely fitted pearls and jewels. One caution: you'll have to be careful, when you cut the string, that you don't let too many beads fall

Wrights metallic trims:

Puff Braid

Rick-Rack

Soutache Braid

Narrow Cord

Medium Cord

Gimp Wave Braid

Large Double "E" Loop Braid

Loop Braid Edging

Bow Tied Braid

Gimp Wheat Pattern

Gimp Galloon

Shell Braid

Plaited Gimp

Cord Chain

Gimp Fringe

Mock Crystal Gimp Scallop Bra

Fringe with Heading

Chinese Braid

Gimp Braid Edging

off the end. If you're quick to catch the end of the string and paste it in place, you'll have no trouble. The two or three pearls which do fall off can be saved and used where needed.

GLOSSARY OF FABRIC TRIMMING TERMS

The language used for describing braids is so technical that most mail-order catalogs simply picture the fabrics, give them a number (numbers differ from catalog to catalog) and let it go at that. Here, however, are some basic terms, mostly generic ones, for those who like to know something about what they're buying. Most trims can be found at trimming counters. Be sure that the metallic ones are non-tarnishable.

BRAID. A trimming made by intertwining or weaving together different strands or cords. Braids are often named for their use or appearance as rosebud braid, etc.

BULLION or purls. Flexible, hollow spiral tubes of gold, silver, or color, made of tiny wires. *Frieze bullion* is rough and sparkly. Available in copper, gold plates, silver plates, aluminum and steel. *Matte bullion* is dull; *shiny bullion* is extremely smooth and satiny.

CORDS, CORDING OR CORDINETTE. A string or small rope of threads twisted together.

FRINGE. Loose threads of fabric on a band of the same material.

GALLOON. A narrow tapelike trimming of rich material.

GIMP. (guimpe). A narrow ornamental trimming fabric often twisted around a metallic wire.

PENDANT. An ornament suspended from a trimming.

PLATE. Flattened, continuous metal strip, usually smooth and brilliant. Available in green, pink, chartreuse, rose and red. Use Eastman 910 to bond this heavy trimming to the egg.

RIBBONETTES. Flat, plaited metallic ribbons available in silver, golds, copper, blue, green, pinks, purple and multicolor.

RICKRACK. Openwork edging made of serpentine braid.

ROPE. A cord made of strands of fiber twisted or braided together.

SEQUINS. An ornamental metal disc or spangle. Sold to egg crafters by the yard.

SOUTACHE. A decorative braid made in varying widths. Sometimes known as Russian braid. Usually narrowly rounded or flat and often in a herringbone twist.

STICK-TO (self-adhesive trimmings). Don't use them or use them only with added glue.

TASSEL. A hanging ornament or ribbon with a tuft or fringe of loose threads or cords.

TWISTS. Threads twisted together to form a rope. Available in medium, heavy and fine textures, and in gold, antique gold, silver, steel, copper and aluminum mixtures. Also in metallic combinations.

WRIGHTS TRIMS. Brand name for decorative trimmings found at trimming counters. Chinese braid 9887 is one of my favorites, as is narrow tubular cord 9917. Both are metallic and, like all Wrights metallics, are non-tarnishable.

BASES AND STANDS

A base or stand adds dignity, importance and of course balance, to the egg. Be sure that the base you use is a decorating asset, selecting it in a texture, color or period to complement your theme. It must be exactly right in size, scale and proportion for its subject, and whether it is an Oriental teakwood *objet d'art* in itself, or a natural piece of driftwood, it should give a sense of completion and stability to your egg.

People who know nothing about egging are always surprised to learn how many, many egg bases are manufactured commercially. These, of course, being planned to hold eggs, are made in the right sizes for the purpose

Lucite stands, grooved to hold eggs, are on the market, and very pretty they are with silvery egg decorations. Use Eastman 910 on the rim of the grooves and set the egg in place. It will dry perfectly clear (other glues leave opaque marks).

However, some of my most valued stands are those which are adapted and converted to serve this purpose. Napkin rings (wooden and metal), candle holders, stones, marble pieces, and driftwood can be used, but by keeping my eyes open for possibilities whenever I shop, I have found donkey carts, glass-dish containers, and all manner of lovely egg accessories and stands.

At the risk of being tiresome, I want to repeat one rule from the design chapter: be sure that any material you use has *at least* one element in common with the other units of the design. If your egg is lined in red, and trimmed in gold, consider a base which has both red and gold, rather than green and silver. If necessary, change the finish on a stand by painting it, glazing it, or otherwise altering it to suit the rest of the composition.

To silver any base, first apply a liquid silver leaf and let dry about 20 minutes. Then apply a coat of decoupage sealer.

Plate 29.   A simple blown chicken egg (left) has been painted with
four coats of red lacquer and a bauble glued to its top. The egg is
then glued to its permanent base, which is about the size of an
egg cup.

The center egg, in pink lacquer, is a center-cut jewel box. The
only trim is the edging of gold cord, one row of 1½mm pearls and
one more row of the gold cord. I found a lovely pink pin among
my grandmother's antique jewelry that was the same shade of pink. It
was exactly right on the front. The stone in its dainty gold setting
was glued with Eastman 910. Seven coats of lacquer were required
for this beautiful finish.

The small araucana chicken egg (right) is not as difficult to
hinge as a chicken egg from other breeds would be. I colored it blue
and trimmed it much the same as the pink goose egg, only I used a
small 3mm gold filigree ball on top.

Plate 30. *The words "bases" and "stands" are used interchangeably. Either one is meant to be a foundation. For egg crafters, there are endless choices. The bases above are just a few samples. They range from short and squat to tall and elegant. They are as simple as the ring form, or as complex as the bears or the tree -like form below, meant to hold a fairly large egg.*

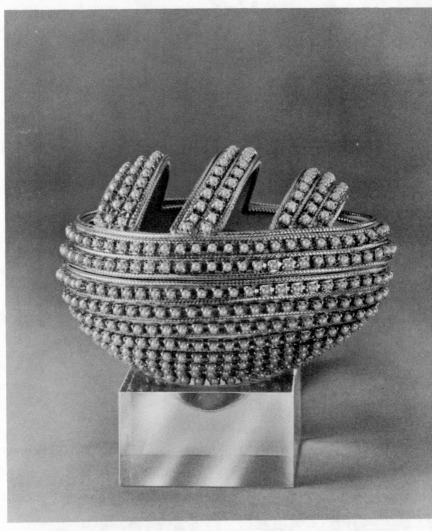

Plate 31. *Another kind of jewel box is similar to the lattice cut, but has fewer sections and the center bar has been eliminated. (Follow the cutting directions but make obvious adjustments.) I covered this egg with row upon row of Tiffany-type pearls, each row separated with silver cord. Notice that there is a double row of cord which indicates where the lid joins the bottom. I used emerald green lining for an interesting contrast to the silver and pearls. The plain lucite base was chosen to reflect the silver and pearls.*

Cameos and small paintings on ceramics make stunning door or inside-the-egg decorations. See plate 17 for an attractive example.

The main point about using these insets is that you plan their inclusion at the very beginning, because your cut must be made with their size clearly in mind.

Cabochons are nothing more nor less than colored glass and stone which imitate precious gems. Today they also refer to a type of convex cut into which stones are polished. Cabochons were used by the French in their most elegant bibelots as long ago as the thirteenth century, which is, I think, a clear license to modern-day egg buffs to go and do likewise.

APPLYING CERAMICS, LARGE STONES, ETC.

Step One. There's no problem at all to securing cameos, stones, etc. to the egg: use Eastman 910. Apply the adhesive to the egg, and then press the ornament firmly in place on the egg. Select a cord trimming that frames your painting, exactly as you would choose a frame for any picture, in the right scale so that it does not overpower the miniature.

painted stone

navette

octagon

square

baguette

"TIFFANY" setting...
prongs hold thick flat-back stones

pear

147

Step Two. It might be a bit tricky for you to spread the glue on the egg in a wide enough area to grip the edges of the ceramic ornament, without having glue show on the decorated surface. Cut out a paper pattern the exact size of the ornament, then trim 1/16-inch off all sides of the pattern. Lay the pattern on the egg and mark the area where glue is to be spread and be careful not to go beyond these marked areas.

Step Three. If the surface of the stone, cameo or ceramic painting doesn't butt right up against the egg, that is, if gaps show, fill in the gaps with little bits of the cord you're using for decoration and trim. By using the same cord as you plan to use on the rest of the egg, you minimize the possibility that the "mechanics" will show.

Many of your eggs will be designed for specific room settings, perhaps with a particular niche, table, stand or tray in mind. For unity, try to relate the decorated egg to its background. A brilliant egg on a lucite stand could lend sparkle and homogenity to the large glass coffee tables so popular today. The lining of the egg could repeat the color of an accent pillow on the sofa. Or your table appointments could have as their common element gold or silver. A theme would be an equally valid harmonizing unit: maybe a tableful of objects from the orient, with an ivory buddha in a lacquered egg as the center of interest?

Ideally, eggs with filigreed windows should be placed so that light comes from behind them to silhouette the filigree. Eggs with textured or carved figurines need front lighting. Bookshelves, unless they are brightly lighted from all sides, are not ideal showcases for most eggs, because the lacquered finishes, the gleaming braids and trims, and the inlaid jewels should sparkle and shine, which they won't do in the dark shelf.

A see-through box imported from Mexico is widely available today in many different sizes, with and without shelves. It makes a pretty, dust-free case for a decorated egg. Don't use doors on the egg, they'll just get in the way of the box opening. Also use a base which is rather low, chunky and flat, not high and leggy. The latter kind tends to look too busy and unrelated to the box.

For big collections, you can find lighted étageres, both glass shelved and mirror-lined.

149

Plate 32. (Opposite)   Before I discovered Eastman 910. I would bolt the hinges on to the thick shells. But the adhesive simplifies the task tremendously. I also use it for applying larger stones to the shell, and for securing the heavy egg to its base.

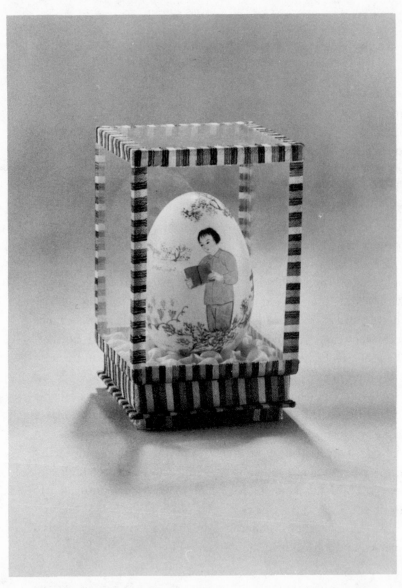

Plate 33.   An ordinary chicken egg—a gift from a friend—is delicately hand-painted in a traditional oriental design, but its setting is quite modern. The box is made from striped corner sections taped to the glass to hold them together.

ͼͼͼͼͼͼͼͼͼͼͼͼͼͼͼͼͼͼͼͼͼͼͼͼͼͼͼͼͼͼ

Egg Decorating That Children Can Do

"And he who gives a child a treat, makes joy-bells ring in Heaven's street."
— John Masefield, *The Everlasting Mercy*

THE DECORATED EGG IS NO LONGER A SEASONAL CRAFT, NOR IS IT only for adults. Children love to work with eggs the year round, and find it a stimulating, creative and educational experience. Teaching young people to select small-scaled materials (many can be "found" objects culled from the family scrapbag or backyard), plan colors, and apply their skill and imagination to using a familiar object in a completely new way makes this an exceptionally worthwhile project for classrooms, nature study programs, and scout meetings.

HOW TO EMPTY AN EGG

Chicken eggs are recommended for children for many reasons. They are inexpensive, easily obtained and emptied, as well as fun to decorate. (Extend the lesson in thrift by making arrangements to use the egg contents — the cooking teacher might be grateful to have a supply?)

151

Step One. Poke a hole in each end of the egg, using a large darning needle or a nail. Enlarge one hole with the point of the needle.

Step Two. Blow into the smaller hole, allowing the contents to run out of the larger hole and into a basin. If the egg does not run freely, poke the needle deep into the yolk to break it.

Step Three. Drip clear tap water into one hole and blow it through the egg. This washes out anything that may have been left inside.

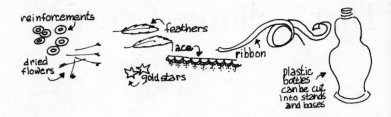

MATERIALS FOR TRIMMING

The very best way to stimulate imagination is to ask the young eggers to collect their own materials from every possible source: nature, pantry, stationery drawer, sewing room, etc.

You'll be surprised at their inventiveness when they've collected an array like this:

Split peas, dry corn kernels, cloves, barley, dried beans and small seeds, dried grasses and corn husks, seed pod pieces, sections of cones, feathers, and scraps from mother's dried flower arrangement. Looseleaf reinforcements (make great eyes), gold stars, Christmas or other seals, tiny buttons, ribbon, lace, braid and string, and anything else they may scrounge from kitchen shelf, desk drawer or garbage pail.

When using paint on the eggs, its best *not* to use a water-base product. I know it's harder to remove oil paints from hands but the oilbase paint (or airplane lacquer) will adhere better and

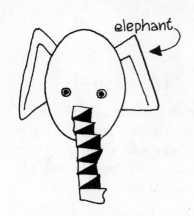

elephant

accordianfold paper "trunk"

the older children will enjoy using it more. Children often become dismayed when their efforts are unsuccessful. I also recommend colored marking pens for younger children who can not handle brushes. The colors dry rapidly, there is a wide range of colors, and it's easy to apply — all of which adds to the enjoyment. And, they can learn by mixing their own colors.

Using paste, the child can add trims, change his mind, and replace it with another quite easily. Children change their minds often, so that a quick-bonding glue could cause problems.

Simple cutout arms, ears, nose or legs can change an egg to an animal or a person in just minutes. Most children lose interest quickly if the egg decorating becomes too involved. Prepare plenty of eggs in advance, with extras for breakage.

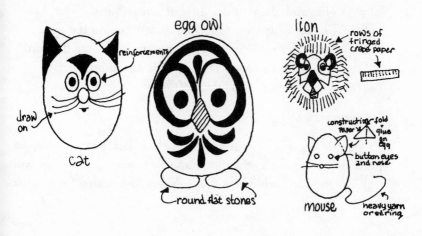

draw on

cat

egg owl

reinforcements

round flat stones

lion

rows of fringed crepe paper

constructing fold
paper glue an egg

button eyes and nose

mouse

heavy yarn or string

WORKING WITH STYROFOAM EGGS

The styrofoam egg is excellent to use wherever the natural egg would be too fragile. The range of finished products is very wide, from decorative to practical pieces, and all are simple to do. Styrofoam is durable and trims can be fastened with pins as well as with glue, making it practical for children to use.

TO DECORATE WITH FOIL

The decorative foil egg is very popular. To make one, you need only a few simple materials:

Styrofoam egg (of any size)
Art foil, very thin quality
Cord or string
Spray adhesive or Elmer's glue
Toothbrush
Soft cloth
Varnish

Step One. Cut a piece of thin art foil large enough to cover the styrofoam egg. Round off the corners. Or, cut strips in various shapes and sizes.

Step Two. Spray the back of the foil with adhesive or use Elmer's glue and allow to dry at least ten minutes.

Step Three. Glue cord to form a design around the egg.

Step Four. Place foil around the egg, directly over the cord.

Step Five. Tap the foil to the egg with a toothbrush.

Step Six. Rub the foil with a soft cloth.

TO ANTIQUE

Antique the egg by painting it with a dark accent color, let paint remain on for five minutes and then wipe it off. This will leave interesting highlights. The egg should be dried for at least six hours before you apply the final coats of varnish (at least four coats will be necessary). Be sure the egg dries thoroughly after each coat.

USES FOR STYROFOAM EGGS

As styrofoam is easy to obtain and relatively inexpensive, it can be used for many things. Many have hollowed-out centers. An unusual egg can be made by placing a scene inside and decorating the outside.

Step One. Covered with fabrics and trims, it makes a pretty pincushion.

Step Two. It can also be the perfect head for a doll.

Step Three. It is practical for it makes unbreakable Christmas ornaments.

Since styrofoam eggs are available in different colors, trim can be added to match the background color of the egg itself.

Many paints and glues do not work well on styrofoam because they erode the egg, leaving large holes. The best glue is Elmer's. Before using spray adhesive, check the label on the can to be sure it is recommended for styrofoam. When adding trims, pins are easier to use than glue. Short pins are preferred for surface trims because they will not penetrate the egg as deeply as the regular length.

STYROFOAM EGG PINCUSHION

This would make an excellent children's project, or a quickly-made item for the bazaar. It is deliberately simple because the addition of the pins would interfere with any extraneous trimmings. The self-adhesive ribbon is found in hobby shops.

Step One. Choose a fairly large styrofoam egg for practicality.

Step Two. You'll need about 2 yards of narrow (½″ or less) velvet, self-adhesive ribbon. Or an assortment of colors that add up to 2 yards.

Step Three. Now, simply remove the backing from the ribbon and start wrapping on the smallest end.

Step Four. Mount it on a wooden napkin ring, with Eastman 910 adhesive.

Step Five. Follow all the steps above except Step 4, to make a Christmas tree ornament. Paste gold medallions on each end for a little glitter, and allow an extra loop of velvet on one end for a hanger.

SCENIC EGG WITH BALLANTINE

For older children only, here's another way to design, using ballantine and tiny pictures.

Step One. Cut a hole in each end of a chicken egg with an X-acto knife. Pour out the contents after the first cut, and clean the egg thoroughly.

Step Two. Cut Saran wrap slightly larger than the openings on each end of the egg, and glue it lightly over the ends.

Step Three. Cover the entire egg with a coat of Elmer's glue, except for the Saran-wrapped ends (use them to hold the egg).

Step Four. Sprinkle Ballantine all over the egg, catching the excess in the lid of a box.

156 *Step Five.* Cover the edge, where the Saran meets the Ballantine, with a trim of gold or other braid trim.

Step Six. Cut a tiny picture and glue it on the outside of each end of the Saran.

9

Egg Dolls, Mosaics And Handbags

"It is computed, that eleven thousand persons have, at several times, suffered death, rather than submit to break their eggs at the smaller end."
— Jonathan Swift, *Gulliver's Travels*

HERE ARE SOME PROJECTS THAT ARE GUARANTEED TO COMPEL attention. There's a doll with a real egg head and she's magnificent . . . an ostrich egg handbag that may look fragile but really isn't . . . and a catastrophe project, that is, what to make from broken eggshells.

DOLLS MADE FROM EGGS

MAKING THE BODY

A fascinating project is the making of dolls with egg heads. The body should be made first, and the appropriately-sized, well-proportioned egg head added later. The body of the doll can be made from fabrics (even remnants will do) and stuffed with cotton. An historical note can be introduced with period dolls dressed in the fashions worn during that era.

157

After completing the body insert a long wire, florist's pick or ordinary stick as far as the waistline of the doll, leaving the remaining portions sticking up through the neck for eventual attachment of the head. Leave sufficient fabric above the body to form the neck, and to attach it to the head.

MAKING THE HEAD

The goose egg, which is so durable, is the best choice for the head, but it is not the only possibility. Whatever your choice, empty the contents through a small hole in the bottom of the egg. Let the cavity dry. Now pour in melted paraffin (or liquid plaster as it is done in the Orient) almost to the top. Let the wax begin to set up (hole up) in an old egg carton. As the wax (or plaster) begins to harden, remove the wire or stick from the body of the doll and insert it through the hole into the egg. Let it remain there while the wax becomes completely solid.

Now put the head on the doll by inserting the wire or stick back into the body. Poke the head far enough down so that it fits the body well and glue that extra fabric (remember you left some) to the egghead with Duo surgical adhesive.

It is also possible to mount the emptied egg on the body without the wax-and-stick process, but securing it directly with Duo Surgical adhesive. But the doll head is not placed as firmly this way. However, it is a perfectly good method for dolls meant only for decoration, not for play.

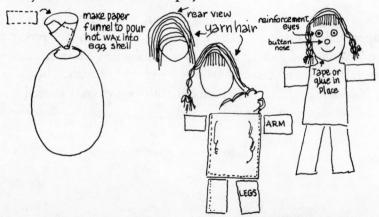

make paper funnel to pour hot wax into egg shell

rear view
yarn hair

reinforcement
eyes
button nose
Tape or glue in place

ARM

LEGS

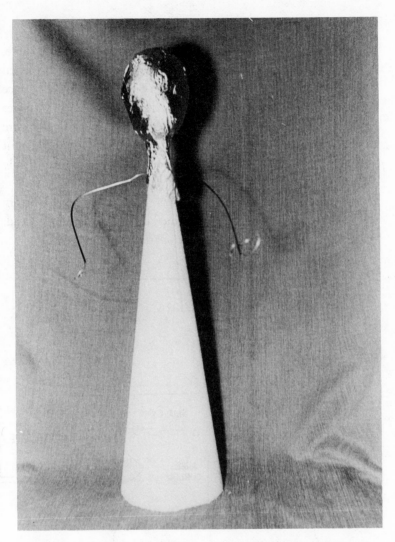

Plate 34. A doll in the process of construction. A styrofoam egg head has been attached to the cone-shaped styrofoam body, and the head and neck covered with foil. The wire protrusions are curled at the ends and roughly shaped. They form the armatures for the arms.

The face can be simple with just lines to indicate eyes, nose, and mouth. Or you may draw the face on the egg with pencil and then fill in the colors with ordinary Testors paint. The face may be painted before the doll is made, but to have the features in the best position, wait until the egg head is dry and secure to the body. The head might even fit on the body at a different angle than planned, and a pre-painted face could end up badly askew.

The hair is made preferably of yarn, but cotton is a satisfactory substitute. Either one should be glued directly to the doll's head. If yarn is used, select a size in proportion to the egg.

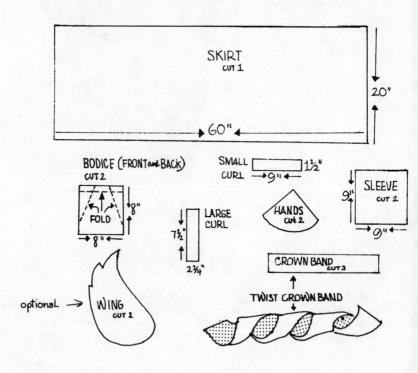

HOLIDAY EGG HEAD DOLL

This elegant doll holding decorated eggs and surrounded by tiny packages is a superb gift. It could be the focal point of your holiday table or of your Christmas décor. Hang decorated eggs on the tree, make an egg wreath (see plate 46) and your holiday theme will be clear to all.

You can make many variations of this doll. Transform her into a beautiful angel by adding wire wings covered with foil. Or crown the top of her head with an Advent wreath and tiny candles and make a Swedish Lucia.

The plastic-backed gold foil (which is used as candy wrapping in France) is sold as Tarzan paper or Leo Paper in the United States. Most floral supply houses and hobbycraft shops sell it. You can make 4 large or 6 small dolls from each roll.

The doll is easily stored from year to year. Merely fluff out her dress from the underside and she'll be as fresh as new. You can drape the foil easily, and it makes no mess whatsoever. Should you want to "tone down" figures, a medium brown floral spray can be applied to the finished figure to highlight the folded areas.

MATERIALS

Gold foil
Gold or silver straight pins
Styrofoam egg 2½" high
Styrofoam cone 10" high
Floral spray
Floral stick
Medium weight floral wire

METHOD:

Step One. Place the egg on top of the cone, securing it by putting a floral stick down into the cone's top, leaving just enough to go through the egg and attach the two pieces. This forms the basic body. Add the wire for the arms, being careful not to place it too low, or the figure will lose her waistline.

Step Two. Cover the head with a square cut from the foil. Just wrap it over the egg and squeeze it on the form. Because of the plastic lining on the foil, it will remain in position without pinning.

Step Three. Measure 1 yard of foil for the skirt. Fold the bottom to make a 1" hem (no pinning necessary). Next close the two ends, making a circle with pins on the underside. If there is a pattern in the foil, do not worry about matching.

Gather the skirt on the cone at the waist, inserting pins into the cone to hold the skirt. It will look quite full at the waist, but simply squeeze it to the form.

Step Four. You are now ready to cover the arms and hands, just enough to give them body. Only the hands will show so give them a more finished look. You need not make fingers — just a suggestion of a hand.

Step Five. Cut two large 6 inch squares, one for the front of the dress, the other for the back. Attach the back piece first and then the front piece can wrap around and be pinned to the side of the figure. If the figure is too flat, simply stuff her with foil scraps. Do not try to hide the pins you use because they will not be noticed when the project is completed.

162

Step Six. Now you are ready to attach the sleeves. Cut two more 6 inch squares of foil, and let your imagination go, designing the sleeve in any way that you like. Attach it partly to the cone and partly to the bodice of the dress, wherever it is most secure.

Step Seven. The last part to be constructed is the hair, and once again your own creativity can come into focus. You can use either a simple style of braided foil, or you can make curls by winding 1 inch strips of foil (5 inches long) around your finger. Perhaps you would like to make a hairdo combining curls and braids. Attach curls and/or braids to the head with pins.

Step Eight. When the construction is completed spray with floral spray, holding the can some distance from the figure and using only enough spray to accent it. (A newspaper background will help you tidy up quickly.)

Step Nine. Add trim. Self-adhesive lace and trimmings (from Wrights) are very nice for this, in that they do not tarnish and are as handsome as Swiss braids. They are available in a large selection of styles.

Hang decorated eggs from doll's hands, and fill her arms with more of the same. The little packages at her feet are made from tiny boxes wrapped in Christmas paper and decorated with odd lengths of braid, and leftover ornaments and trims.

MOSAIC PICTURES

If you've ever made a mosaic picture from seeds, seashells, or tiles, you know how much fun it can be. An egg mosaic can be even more smashing (pun intended). Any time you break an eggshell, store it until you have enough to make a mosaic.

The lighter, more fragile shells of chicken, turkey and duck are used for mosaics, but there's no reason why you can't use some of the harder shells. Whatever you do, select shells of the same thickness for your first mosaic picture. Later you can use materials of varying thicknesses.

Pick a theme for your picture. Point up the theme with trims and accents. Ecclesiastical gold and purple would make a lovely color scheme for a religious subject. Bright yellows and oranges are folksy. Pearls can be included in the theme, or perhaps pieces of broken seashell.

You can make a simple, realistic mosaic designed from the symbols used in Pysanky (see index for page number) or do a modern abstract, with the eggshells, themselves, providing a study in textures.

If you like, you can add seeds, split peas, beans and corn to make a mosaic of all-natural materials. If you do use these I suggest that you have all the colors the same (let's say an all-white design); otherwise, the mosaic would lack unity.

Also, if you wish, you can leave part of the board background exposed to make a less ambitious project. The exposed part of the board could be painted.

METHOD FOR MAKING MOSAICS

Step One. Prepare a piece of canvas board, masonite, or even heavy cardboard and lightly sketch in your design.

Step Two. Now prepare the eggshells. Crush them to the desired texture and size. You can paint the shells if you wish (now or later) or use different shell colors (white, brown, speckled) to form the picture.

Step Three. Apply Elmer's glue sparingly to a small area on the board. If you use too much glue, it will ooze out and make the mosaic messy.

Step Four. Fill in your design using bits and pieces of irregular shells, rather as though you were putting together a jigsaw puzzle. Break off ends of shells where you like. Overlap some; keep others adjacent. Tweezers will help you lay the pieces in place.

Step Five. After all the pieces of shell are glued in position, you can paint your design on each piece of shell, one at a time (to make it easy to make changes!).

Step Six. Now, if you like, grout may be carefully rubbed over the entire board, filling in the spaces between individual pieces of shell. When the grout has dried, you can just brush away any excess. You can buy grout already mixed wherever ceramic tiles are sold (at paint and hobby stores, for example). Grout also comes powdered, to be mixed with water as directed on the package. The grout will make a smooth white texture contrast for the luminous shells.

Step Seven. Although the natural egg supplies its own porcelain-like finish, it's usually a good idea to intensify the luminosity of the shells and help preserve your work by applying a decoupage sealer as the final step.

HANDBAGS MADE FROM LARGE EGGS

SUITABLE EGGS

I have enjoyed carrying my handbag for years; everyone is astonished to discover that it's really an egg! There are marked limitations to egg selections for the handbag — only the rhea or emu can be used ideally.

1. Cut the egg horizontally exactly through the middle. Before gluing the hinge on the handbag a slight sanding (where the hinge is to be attached) will help the hinge to hold better, especially on the emu egg. The texture of the shell is so rough that the Eastman 910 adhesive is necessary. Follow the directions for making a jewel box; choosing a heavier hinge, latch and chains than you would for a goose egg.

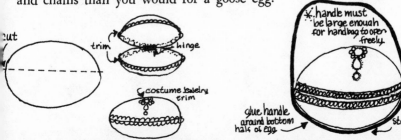

Now that the egg is cut and hinged you are ready for the basic design.

Step One. Start all designs with a simple cord around the opening of the top lid and the bottom of the handbag to stabilize and hold the tirms.

Step Two. Pearls are a lovely contrast on the emu egg, while colored stones show off extremely well on the off-white background of the rhea egg.

Step Three. You can use costume jewelry for trim. I sometimes purchase pins, necklaces, etc., from matching sets for trimming.

Step Four. Select your lining material carefully. Avoid velvets, for they are not as effective as the soft silks. A wild or dark color could spoil the whole effect when the handbag is opened.

Step Five. In attaching the handle of the bag, consider how you are going to carry the bag. Consider the size of the bag also. The first handle I made was simply a one inch braid from my work table. That is the handle that shows in the photograph of the handbag. It has held up well and has been easy to hold. Another good choice would be a choker necklace. I tried a bracelet, but it was too small. A longer necklace can be shortened to fit by removing several links. If you have to do this, be sure to purchase a type of necklace or chain that is easy to work with. Attach the handle with Eastman 910 adhesive.

Line the handbag egg, using the method described for the jewel box egg. However, two chains are advisable to prevent undue pressure on the hinge.

A final touch — glue a tiny round or oval mirror into the lid using Eastman 910 adhesive. Frame mirror with cord.

10

How To Price Eggs For Sale

". . . half a trade and half an art."
— W. R. Inge, *The Victorian Age*

MANY TIMES I HAVE BEEN ASKED HOW TO PRICE AN EGG. IT'S NOT easy!

First consider the cost of the egg itself. A goose egg could cost from fifty cents to several dollars, depending on where and how it is purchased. Many goose eggs are too small to be used for eggs with a door. The inexpensive duck egg is useful when it's necessary to keep the price low. On the other hand, an ostrich egg can cost from seven to twenty-five dollars, depending again on the source. So, begin with the cost of the basic egg. Next add the cost of the trim, the base, and any figures inside. To this total, add the approximate value of your time. I've heard many egging friends say their time isn't worth much. While it may be difficult to figure what the dollar amount is, it must be a significant factor in estimating the total value of the egg.

It is obvious that some eggs take far longer than others to do, and the prices should reflect this difference. It is not necessary to keep a strict record for each egg, but even if you are working

167

on several eggs simultaneously, going back and forth from one to another, you should be able to allot the time spent on each. When I first started designing eggs, I valued my time at five dollars an hour. This was for an egg that developed from the materials at hand on my work table without additional design drawings. Now I make or create only one-of-a-kind eggs. Much more complex in the planning, and much more time-consuming is locating the material necessary to carry out each individual theme; this egg must be more expensive. The development of an original idea from the first thought, through all the stages, to the finished product has always been, and always will be, more costly.

PHOTOGRAPHING EGGS FOR YOUR FILES

No matter how many eggs you make, it is wise to photograph, and keep a record of each one. I must admit I did not do this at first, and so I have no visual record of some of my early designs. A simple flash picture will be adequate, but it should be made with color film. Keep the pictures in a file, preferably separating them into categories — jewel boxes, single-door eggs, double-door eggs, etc. It will be a valuable record of your work and a good reference file.

BE A GOOD CRAFTSMAN

Gather all your materials and information on sources for materials and eggs, in addition to the file of photographs I have just mentioned.

Be clean, tidy and well-organized as you work ... dust (it can't be mentioned too often) spells disaster to a fine finish.

Be original, even radical, in your designs but conservative in the amount of decoration you add. If you have any doubt about whether the egg really needs more trim, *it probably doesn't!* Too much trim will take away from the simple shape and beauty of the egg.

QUALITY CONTROL

When making eggs for show or sale, have quality control. Set certain standards for yourself and live up to them. Because of your high standards, people will recognize you as a reputable craftsman. Start by building a clientele, let people know about your work and make certain that quality rather than quantity prevails.

SIGNED EGGS

Sign every important egg, whether you make it for yourself or to give. An unsigned egg is like an unsigned painting. The signature adds not only the final touch of the artist but also value to the egg. Since the egg will be the heirloom of tomorrow — a signature, initials or some sort of trademark is essential.

I add my signature on the bottom of the egg, using India ink. Then I protect it with a coat of decoupage sealer. For costlier eggs, a small metal name plate reading "A Rosemary Disney Egg" is wired to the base or stand.

EGG-CRAFT HOW-TO FOR THE BAZAAR COMMITTEE

Eggs make fast-selling bazaar items in any season, but you should do especially well with tree ornaments timed for a pre-holiday sale. For gift items, the jewel boxes, eggs with surprises inside, or any other beautifully decorated egg will bring a good profit and publicity for the bazaar as well. Why not auction off the most beautiful one of all?

1. Advance planning pays dividends. A year ahead is not too soon. Even with a lot of willing hands, you'll need 6 months.

2. Show a few samples of finished eggs; if possible, at the first meeting, and demonstrate how each one is made. See Plate 19.

3. Organize a good committee of craftsmen as well as "leggers" (those who will locate, donate or pick-up supplies). Let the leggers go to work immediately with a list of supplies needed. Choose a leader, too. Somebody must keep track of everything.

4. Fit out a portable box to tote all supplies to and from meetings. Items like glues, scissors, a cutting tool, trims, paints, etc. should be included.

5. Have workers creating at every meeting. Wonders can be accomplished with an assembly line technique. But don't discourage any who want to work at home, alone.

6. Have your leggers round up plastic bags or boxes for completed items. Not only will boxes keep things fresh, but they will make an attractive display at bazaar time.

7. Take orders on more elaborate designs . . . but be sure to make quantities of all things that promise to be fast sellers (such as inexpensive gift items made of styrofoam eggs). You may not have enough time left to take orders at the bazaar and still fill them by the holidays.

170

8. Try something new: perhaps you might want to precut eggs and sell them (or an assembled kit!) to hobbyists. Why not have someone demonstrating one or more of the decorating methods at your booth to step up sales?

9. When pricing items, don't forget your hours of labor.

10. Display your items on a plain background and do not crowd them. A good way is to display items on different levels by borrowing lazy susans, trays on stands, some hanging device, or a suitable make-believe Christmas tree. And, if yours is a Spring Fair, make a colorful "egg tree" following directions in chapter 11.

A mushroom scene in a driftwood base (see page 116 for treating wood) is made from inexpensive materials — good for a bazaar. Cut chicken eggs in half with an X-acto knife and paint with water-colors — one streaked with blue, one beige, one dark-brown speckles. Mount as shown in figure.

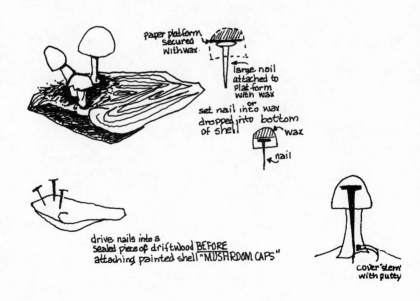

11

Egg Designs For Gifts And Special Occasions

"The only gift is a portion of thyself."
— Ralph Waldo Emerson

Whenever you celebrate a special day, the splendid egg is ready to participate in one of its many guises. Bring one beautifully decorated egg to a birthday party as the gift for the honored guest, turn another into a novel centerpiece, or fancy-up a dozen eggs for table favors or place markers.

While Easter is the holiday most closely associated with egg decorating and egg gifts, with a simple change of theme the "Easter" egg can become·a delightful Valentine, a centerpiece at the Thanksgiving banquet, a miniature bassinette for a birth announcement, a Christmas tree ornament or the crowning touch on a wedding cake.

Plate 35. What an exciting gift this double-door egg would make for a little boy's birthday! Think of his delight when he opens the little doors to find the wooden soldiers standing at attention in the guardhouse and in each door. Care was taken, in designing this egg, that everything would fit, and the doors close properly. The double flower base is appropriate and inexpensive. A plain gold cord edges the opening and trims the inside of the doors. Granted this is a fragile gift, every little boy has a special place for keeping treasures.

Plate 36. *The point in the Queen Anne cut offers the perfect setting for a birthstone. All coats of paint should be completed before you add the stone. Birthstone symbols for each month are:*

January: Garnet
February: Amethyst
March: Aquamarine,
    Bloodstone
April: Diamond
May: Emerald
June: Pearl, Moonstone,
    Alexandrite

July: Ruby
August: Peridot, Sardonyx
September: Sapphire
October: Opal, Tourmaline
November: Topaz
December: Turquoise, Zircon,
    Lapis lazuli

Plate 37A and B. *Something very special for the man in your life is this unusual turtle design jewel box, shown open and closed. It started with a goose egg cut with a single door. The commercial turtle base is inexpensive unless you elect to have it gold-plated. After hingeing the door, I placed the door section onto the turtle stand, leaving the rest of the egg to make the high dome of the turtle's back. Would you ever guess that I used the shed skin of an indigo rattler (supplied by a friend who raises snakes)? It contoured nicely because it was paper-thin. The only trim is gold bullion around the cut edges. I used decoupage sealer for a protective finish. If you can't find a snake which just happens to be shedding, you can substitute suede or paint (or marbleize) the shell and trim it quite simply. I lined the top and bottom of this jewel box in dark silk (just once breaking my rule about using light colors for linings), and presented it complete with cuff links.*

Incidentally, Henry Fonda owns this turtle egg and several others that I have designed.

Plate 38. Eggs with a Zodiac theme are surely the most personalized of gifts. This basic jewel box cut is simply trimmed and painted so that the Zodiac sign stands out boldly. Here are the astrological themes for which you might find appropriate figures, bases, ornaments, prints, etc.

Aries (Ram): March 21-
   April 20
Taurus (Bull): April 21-
   May 20
Gemini (Twins): May 21-
   June 21
Cancer (Crab): June 22-
   July 22
Leo (Lion): July 23-
   August 23
Virgo (Virgin): August 24-
   September 22

Libra (Scale): September 23-
   October 23
Scorpio (Scorpion): October
   24-November 22
Sagittarius (Hunter and
   Bow): November 23-
   December 21
Capricorn (Goat): December
   22-January 19
Aquarius (Water): January
   20-February 18
Pisces (Fish): February 19-
   March 20

Plate 39. (Opposite) Elegant silver and sparkling pearls encircle a jewel box goose egg that would make a peerless Silver Anniversary gift. Under all that splendor, I first applied a coat of Testor's silver paint to take care of any gaps that might occur in the trim stage. I trimmed the bottom half first, covering the opening edge with silver bullion and then a row of 2mm pearls. I repeated these two rows three more times. Next came two rows of 1mm pearls alternated with the silver bullion. The tiny pearls add perspective. I stopped short of covering the bottom—there's a tiny oval of the silver paint.

I began trimming the top section with silver roping on the edge, then added one row of a wider twisted cord, a row of rhinestones and another row of the cord. From there on, I alternated twisted cord and 2mm pearls until the top was completely covered. I think the rhinestone cluster on top adds a jaunty touch! The pear-shaped stones come individually attached to silver wire. I twisted a dozen of them together and concealed the ends under a tiny round and flat filigree. White lining and a fine silver chain finished the interior.

Plate 40. Thanksgiving Day may call for a very special thank-you to someone dear—perhaps your hostess or a neighbor. What could be more appropriate than a jewel box made from the delightful speckled turkey egg. This one was lined with (of course!) pumpkin colored silk. The egg stand is really beautiful. It is of sterling silver with gold overlay and was made by Tiffany. From the collection of Dr. and Mrs. James M. Stewart.

Plate 41. Free-standing eggs (that is, eggs which are not seen backed against a wall) should have multi-faceted interest. For this reason, I designed an egg with a filigree window behind the figure. Scenes such as this can be adapted to many different needs and occasions, since a wide variety of human and animal figurines are on the market. I started the trim with a reinforcing cord of gold around the opening and the door. Then I selected a Wrights trimming one-inch wide (the large scale suits the oversize goose egg), with a fretwork pattern that has the quality of the filigree. I then added another row of gold cording. The stand echoed the openwork pattern. Collection of Dr. and Mrs. Harold Bales.

Plate 42.   A hanging garden is an instant attraction, especially when it's thriving in a surprise planter, such as an ostrich egg in a macramé holder. Even if you have ungreen thumbs, you can easily grow a splendid collection of foliage in tap water. Just cut a new tip-end branch of coleus, English ivy, philodendron, nephthytis (arrowhead), pick-a-back plant, pothos, or, even an African violet leaf. Put it in water in the egg with a piece of charcoal to keep the water sweet. Plants should root quickly. Change the water when it gets cloudy and add plant food every two weeks or so. If the egg won't hold water —and sometimes it won't after the membrane is cut—fear not. Just apply a lining of liquid solder, melted paraffin or even polyethylene inside the cleaned egg. Another kind of instant decoration can be yours if you use an egg to hold a dried flower arrangement. Macramé designed by Bert Sabia.

Plate 43. *A Christmas gift that is symbolic, enchanting and hand-made will really become a cherished possession. A large goose egg was used to permit the cutting of double doors in front and two filigree windows in back. The top filigree is set in to create the effect of a halo around the Mexican mother-and-child-figurines. The egg was left entirely natural except for the trim of gold on all cut edges. I used 2½mm pearls on the inner edge of each door, a larger size than usual because I wanted to achieve better balance when the doors are open. From the collection of Adele Richardson.*

Plate 44. *The back of the same egg. These double-filigreed windows are so very reminiscent of church or chapel windows, that I recomment them for occasions which have deep symbolic meaning. A wedding-gift egg with a bride and groom inside could be designed to ornament the wedding cake, then to become a permanent keepsake of the big occasion.*

For this purpose, choose a perfect white egg, preferably a double-yolk goose egg to give enough width for the windows, and use white or silver trim. Usually the filigrees will need no edging, but occasionally small gaps occur which need covering. For this purpose, use gold cord or braid, or, as I did here, gold looping. You will need a base, even for a wedding cake ornament. Conceal the base in the top of the cake and wash it off later.

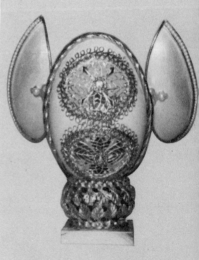

Plate 45. Create your own tradition with a Christmas decoration that might become the family's favorite. It can grace a mantle, or act as a centerpiece. It is very easy to make; but once made it can be stored away from year to year. It also makes a meaningful gift. The small goose egg was left in its natural color. I used the one inch gold braid next to the edging of gold roping and, for a third row, I used the soft gold roping in a larger size than that used for edging. The door is also edged with gold roping.

Plate 46. A Christmas wreath made of eggs may not be just the first in your neighborhood, it might well be the first one in the whole town! Start with the wire frame (available at florist shops and nurseries). Then gather your blown eggs. Most of mine were chicken eggs but I added a few goose eggs and made one of them a golden goose egg. Thread florists wire through the holes in the blown eggs. Secure each one to the wire frame. Fill in as you go with real or artificial greens, also wired to the frame. I added a bright red bow for my last touch. The wreath pictured graced my front door this past holiday season, so it does withstand the weather. For a touch of humor, you might want to add a toy goose beside the golden egg. The neighborhood children will love it!

Plate 47. The Nativity scene, a favorite Christmas symbol, is permitted by most churches. I used stylized wood figures and repeated the wood in the trimming beads. The egg is an ostrich egg with a single door. The opening is outlined as usual with gold cord, then Wrights Chinese braid, and then a strip of gold rolled cord. Next I 185 glued on 6mm wooden beads all the way around. The door needed only one row of the rolled braid. It is lined in soft blue brocade. To accommodate this large egg, I turned the base upside-down. Bases can often be just as attractive upside down as right-side-up.

Plate 48. *A magnificent egg with a Madonna and Child theme will make a memorable Christmas gift. This single door cut is not only richly lined with pearls, but it has a filigree too. The oval filigree is best for use in this way. First hinge the door and tape it back in its position in the egg before you trace and cut the opening for the filigree. The outside of the door has only a rim of gold cord around the edge. The figures are of colored wax. The frame around the opening in the egg is trimmed with gold cord, then a row of one-inch Wrights trim and finally the rolled braid. The base is a double daisy.*

Plate 49. Harvey Dresner, our photographer, hatched this idea—the diaper pin goes in and out of an ordinary chicken egg. It could be fun for a baby-shower place card.

INDEX

A CATALOG OF
SELECTED DOVER BOOKS
IN ALL FIELDS OF INTEREST

A CATALOG OF SELECTED DOVER BOOKS IN ALL FIELDS OF INTEREST

CONCERNING THE SPIRITUAL IN ART, Wassily Kandinsky. Pioneering work by father of abstract art. Thoughts on color theory, nature of art. Analysis of earlier masters. 12 illustrations. 80pp. of text. 5⅜ × 8½. 23411-8 Pa. $2.50

LEONARDO ON THE HUMAN BODY, Leonardo da Vinci. More than 1200 of Leonardo's anatomical drawings on 215 plates. Leonardo's text, which accompanies the drawings, has been translated into English. 506pp. 8⅜ × 11¾. 24483-0 Pa. $10.95

GOBLIN MARKET, Christina Rossetti. Best-known work by poet comparable to Emily Dickinson, Alfred Tennyson. With 46 delightfully grotesque illustrations by Laurence Housman. 64pp. 4 × 6¾. 24516-0 Pa. $2.50

THE HEART OF THOREAU'S JOURNALS, edited by Odell Shepard. Selections from *Journal*, ranging over full gamut of interests. 228pp. 5⅜ × 8½. 20741-2 Pa. $4.50

MR. LINCOLN'S CAMERA MAN: MATHEW B. BRADY, Roy Meredith. Over 300 Brady photos reproduced directly from original negatives, photos. Lively commentary. 368pp. 8⅜ × 11¼. 23021-X Pa. $11.95

PHOTOGRAPHIC VIEWS OF SHERMAN'S CAMPAIGN, George N. Barnard. Reprint of landmark 1866 volume with 61 plates: battlefield of New Hope Church, the Etawah Bridge, the capture of Atlanta, etc. 80pp. 9 × 12. 23445-2 Pa. $6.00

A SHORT HISTORY OF ANATOMY AND PHYSIOLOGY FROM THE GREEKS TO HARVEY, Dr. Charles Singer. Thoroughly engrossing non-technical survey. 270 illustrations. 211pp. 5⅜ × 8½. 20389-1 Pa. $4.50

REDOUTE ROSES IRON-ON TRANSFER PATTERNS, Barbara Christopher. Redouté was botanical painter to the Empress Josephine; transfer his famous roses onto fabric with these 24 transfer patterns. 80pp. 8¼ × 10⅞. 24292-7 Pa. $3.50

THE FIVE BOOKS OF ARCHITECTURE, Sebastiano Serlio. Architectural milestone, first (1611) English translation of Renaissance classic. Unabridged reproduction of original edition includes over 300 woodcut illustrations. 416pp. 9⅜ × 12¼. 24349-4 Pa. $14.95

CARLSON'S GUIDE TO LANDSCAPE PAINTING, John F. Carlson. Authoritative, comprehensive guide covers, every aspect of landscape painting. 34 reproductions of paintings by author; 58 explanatory diagrams. 144pp. 8⅜ × 11. 22927-0 Pa. $4.95

101 PUZZLES IN THOUGHT AND LOGIC, C.R. Wylie, Jr. Solve murders, robberies, see which fishermen are liars—purely by reasoning! 107pp. 5⅜ × 8½. 20367-0 Pa. $2.00

TEST YOUR LOGIC, George J. Summers. 50 more truly new puzzles with new turns of thought, new subtleties of inference. 100pp. 5⅜ × 8½. 22877-0 Pa. $2.25

THE MURDER BOOK OF J.G. REEDER, Edgar Wallace. Eight suspenseful stories by bestselling mystery writer of 20s and 30s. Features the donnish Mr. J.G. Reeder of Public Prosecutor's Office. 128pp. 5⅜ × 8½. (Available in U.S. only)
24374-5 Pa. $3.50

ANNE ORR'S CHARTED DESIGNS, Anne Orr. Best designs by premier needlework designer, all on charts: flowers, borders, birds, children, alphabets, etc. Over 100 charts, 10 in color. Total of 40pp. 8¼ × 11.   23704-4 Pa. $2.25

BASIC CONSTRUCTION TECHNIQUES FOR HOUSES AND SMALL BUILDINGS SIMPLY EXPLAINED, U.S. Bureau of Naval Personnel. Grading, masonry, woodworking, floor and wall framing, roof framing, plastering, tile setting, much more. Over 675 illustrations. 568pp. 6½ × 9¼.   20242-9 Pa. $8.95

MATISSE LINE DRAWINGS AND PRINTS, Henri Matisse. Representative collection of female nudes, faces, still lifes, experimental works, etc., from 1898 to 1948. 50 illustrations. 48pp. 8⅜ × 11¼.   23877-6 Pa. $2.50

HOW TO PLAY THE CHESS OPENINGS, Eugene Znosko-Borovsky. Clear, profound examinations of just what each opening is intended to do and how opponent can counter. Many sample games. 147pp. 5⅜ × 8½.   22795-2 Pa. $2.95

DUPLICATE BRIDGE, Alfred Sheinwold. Clear, thorough, easily followed account: rules, etiquette, scoring, strategy, bidding; Goren's point-count system, Blackwood and Gerber conventions, etc. 158pp. 5⅜ × 8½.   22741-3 Pa. $3.00

SARGENT PORTRAIT DRAWINGS, J.S. Sargent. Collection of 42 portraits reveals technical skill and intuitive eye of noted American portrait painter, John Singer Sargent. 48pp. 8¼ × 11⅛.   24524-1 Pa. $2.95

ENTERTAINING SCIENCE EXPERIMENTS WITH EVERYDAY OBJECTS, Martin Gardner. Over 100 experiments for youngsters. Will amuse, astonish, teach, and entertain. Over 100 illustrations. 127pp. 5⅜ × 8½.   24201-3 Pa. $2.50

TEDDY BEAR PAPER DOLLS IN FULL COLOR: A Family of Four Bears and Their Costumes, Crystal Collins. A family of four Teddy Bear paper dolls and nearly 60 cut-out costumes. Full color, printed one side only. 32pp. 9¼ × 12¼.
24550-0 Pa. $3.50

NEW CALLIGRAPHIC ORNAMENTS AND FLOURISHES, Arthur Baker. Unusual, multi-useable material: arrows, pointing hands, brackets and frames, ovals, swirls, birds, etc. Nearly 700 illustrations. 80pp. 8⅜ × 11¼.
24095-9 Pa. $3.75

DINOSAUR DIORAMAS TO CUT & ASSEMBLE, M. Kalmenoff. Two complete three-dimensional scenes in full color, with 31 cut-out animals and plants. Excellent educational toy for youngsters. Instructions; 2 assembly diagrams. 32pp. 9¼ × 12¼.   24541-1 Pa. $3.95

SILHOUETTES: A PICTORIAL ARCHIVE OF VARIED ILLUSTRATIONS, edited by Carol Belanger Grafton. Over 600 silhouettes from the 18th to 20th centuries. Profiles and full figures of men, women, children, birds, animals, groups and scenes, nature, ships, an alphabet. 144pp. 8⅜ × 11¼.   23781-8 Pa. $4.95

25 KITES THAT FLY, Leslie Hunt. Full, easy-to-follow instructions for kites made from inexpensive materials. Many novelties. 70 illustrations. 110pp. 5⅜ × 8½.
22550-X Pa. $2.25

PIANO TUNING, J. Cree Fischer. Clearest, best book for beginner, amateur. Simple repairs, raising dropped notes, tuning by easy method of flattened fifths. No previous skills needed. 4 illustrations. 201pp. 5⅜ × 8½.   23267-0 Pa. $3.50

EARLY AMERICAN IRON-ON TRANSFER PATTERNS, edited by Rita Weiss. 75 designs, borders, alphabets, from traditional American sources. 48pp. 8¼ × 11.
23162-3 Pa. $1.95

CROCHETING EDGINGS, edited by Rita Weiss. Over 100 of the best designs for these lovely trims for a host of household items. Complete instructions, illustrations. 48pp. 8¼ × 11.   24031-2 Pa. $2.25

FINGER PLAYS FOR NURSERY AND KINDERGARTEN, Emilie Poulsson. 18 finger plays with music (voice and piano); entertaining, instructive. Counting, nature lore, etc. Victorian classic. 53 illustrations. 80pp. 6½ × 9¼. 22588-7 Pa. $1.95

BOSTON THEN AND NOW, Peter Vanderwarker. Here in 59 side-by-side views are photographic documentations of the city's past and present. 119 photographs. Full captions. 122pp. 8¼ × 11.   24312-5 Pa. $6.95

CROCHETING BEDSPREADS, edited by Rita Weiss. 22 patterns, originally published in three instruction books 1939-41. 39 photos, 8 charts. Instructions. 48pp. 8¼ × 11.   23610-2 Pa. $2.00

HAWTHORNE ON PAINTING, Charles W. Hawthorne. Collected from notes taken by students at famous Cape Cod School; hundreds of direct, personal *apercus*, ideas, suggestions. 91pp. 5⅜ × 8½.   20653-X Pa. $2.50

THERMODYNAMICS, Enrico Fermi. A classic of modern science. Clear, organized treatment of systems, first and second laws, entropy, thermodynamic potentials, etc. Calculus required. 160pp. 5⅜ × 8½.   60361-X Pa. $4.00

TEN BOOKS ON ARCHITECTURE, Vitruvius. The most important book ever written on architecture. Early Roman aesthetics, technology, classical orders, site selection, all other aspects. Morgan translation. 331pp. 5⅜ × 8½. 20645-9 Pa. $5.50

THE CORNELL BREAD BOOK, Clive M. McCay and Jeanette B. McCay. Famed high-protein recipe incorporated into breads, rolls, buns, coffee cakes, pizza, pie crusts, more. Nearly 50 illustrations. 48pp. 8¼ × 11.   23995-0 Pa. $2.00

THE CRAFTSMAN'S HANDBOOK, Cennino Cennini. 15th-century handbook, school of Giotto, explains applying gold, silver leaf; gesso; fresco painting, grinding pigments, etc. 142pp. 6⅛ × 9¼.   20054-X Pa. $3.50

FRANK LLOYD WRIGHT'S FALLINGWATER, Donald Hoffmann. Full story of Wright's masterwork at Bear Run, Pa. 100 photographs of site, construction, and details of completed structure. 112pp. 9¼ × 10.   23671-4 Pa. $6.50

OVAL STAINED GLASS PATTERN BOOK, C. Eaton. 60 new designs framed in shape of an oval. Greater complexity, challenge with sinuous cats, birds, mandalas framed in antique shape. 64pp. 8¼ × 11.   24519-5 Pa. $3.50

THE BOOK OF WOOD CARVING, Charles Marshall Sayers. Still finest book for beginning student. Fundamentals, technique; gives 34 designs, over 34 projects for panels, bookends, mirrors, etc. 33 photos. 118pp. 7¾ × 10⅝. 23654-4 Pa. $3.95

CARVING COUNTRY CHARACTERS, Bill Higginbotham. Expert advice for beginning, advanced carvers on materials, techniques for creating 18 projects— mirthful panorama of American characters. 105 illustrations. 80pp. 8⅜ × 11. 24135-1 Pa. $2.50

300 ART NOUVEAU DESIGNS AND MOTIFS IN FULL COLOR, C.B. Grafton. 44 full-page plates display swirling lines and muted colors typical of Art Nouveau. Borders, frames, panels, cartouches, dingbats, etc. 48pp. 9⅜ × 12¼. 24354-0 Pa. $6.00

SELF-WORKING CARD TRICKS, Karl Fulves. Editor of *Pallbearer* offers 72 tricks that work automatically through nature of card deck. No sleight of hand needed. Often spectacular. 42 illustrations. 113pp. 5⅜ × 8½. 23334-0 Pa. $3.50

CUT AND ASSEMBLE A WESTERN FRONTIER TOWN, Edmund V. Gillon, Jr. Ten authentic full-color buildings on heavy cardboard stock in H-O scale. Sheriff's Office and Jail, Saloon, Wells Fargo, Opera House, others. 48pp. 9¼ × 12¼. 23736-2 Pa. $3.95

CUT AND ASSEMBLE AN EARLY NEW ENGLAND VILLAGE, Edmund V. Gillon, Jr. Printed in full color on heavy cardboard stock. 12 authentic buildings in H-O scale: Adams home in Quincy, Mass., Oliver Wight house in Sturbridge, smithy, store, church, others. 48pp. 9¼ × 12¼. 23536-X Pa. $3.95

THE TALE OF TWO BAD MICE, Beatrix Potter. Tom Thumb and Hunca Munca squeeze out of their hole and go exploring. 27 full-color Potter illustrations. 59pp. 4¼ × 5½. (Available in U.S. only) 23065-1 Pa. $1.50

CARVING FIGURE CARICATURES IN THE OZARK STYLE, Harold L. Enlow. Instructions and illustrations for ten delightful projects, plus general carving instructions. 22 drawings and 47 photographs altogether. 39pp. 8⅜ × 11. 23151-8 Pa. $2.50

A TREASURY OF FLOWER DESIGNS FOR ARTISTS, EMBROIDERERS AND CRAFTSMEN, Susan Gaber. 100 garden favorites lushly rendered by artist for artists, craftsmen, needleworkers. Many form frames, borders. 80pp. 8¼ × 11. 24096-7 Pa. $3.50

CUT & ASSEMBLE A TOY THEATER/THE NUTCRACKER BALLET, Tom Tierney. Model of a complete, full-color production of Tchaikovsky's classic. 6 backdrops, dozens of characters, familiar dance sequences. 32pp. 9⅜ × 12¼. 24194-7 Pa. $4.50

ANIMALS: 1,419 COPYRIGHT-FREE ILLUSTRATIONS OF MAMMALS, BIRDS, FISH, INSECTS, ETC., edited by Jim Harter. Clear wood engravings present, in extremely lifelike poses, over 1,000 species of animals. 284pp. 9 × 12. 23766-4 Pa. $9.95

MORE HAND SHADOWS, Henry Bursill. For those at their 'finger ends," 16 more effects—Shakespeare, a hare, a squirrel, Mr. Punch, and twelve more—each explained by a full-page illustration. Considerable period charm. 30pp. 6½ × 9¼. 21384-6 Pa. $1.95

SURREAL STICKERS AND UNREAL STAMPS, William Rowe. 224 haunting, hilarious stamps on gummed, perforated stock, with images of elephants, geisha girls, George Washington, etc. 16pp. one side. 8¼ × 11. 24371-0 Pa. $3.50

GOURMET KITCHEN LABELS, Ed Sibbett, Jr. 112 full-color labels (4 copies each of 28 designs). Fruit, bread, other culinary motifs. Gummed and perforated. 16pp. 8¼ × 11. 24087-8 Pa. $2.95

PATTERNS AND INSTRUCTIONS FOR CARVING AUTHENTIC BIRDS, H.D. Green. Detailed instructions, 27 diagrams, 85 photographs for carving 15 species of birds so life-like, they'll seem ready to fly! 8¼ × 11. 24222-6 Pa. $2.75

FLATLAND, E.A. Abbott. Science-fiction classic explores life of 2-D being in 3-D world. 16 illustrations. 103pp. 5⅜ × 8. 20001-9 Pa. $2.00

DRIED FLOWERS, Sarah Whitlock and Martha Rankin. Concise, clear, practical guide to dehydration, glycerinizing, pressing plant material, and more. Covers use of silica gel. 12 drawings. 32pp. 5⅜ × 8½. 21802-3 Pa. $1.00

EASY-TO-MAKE CANDLES, Gary V. Guy. Learn how easy it is to make all kinds of decorative candles. Step-by-step instructions. 82 illustrations. 48pp. 8¼ × 11. 23881-4 Pa. $2.50

SUPER STICKERS FOR KIDS, Carolyn Bracken. 128 gummed and perforated full-color stickers: GIRL WANTED, KEEP OUT, BORED OF EDUCATION, X-RATED, COMBAT ZONE, many others. 16pp. 8¼ × 11. 24092-4 Pa. $2.50

CUT AND COLOR PAPER MASKS, Michael Grater. Clowns, animals, funny faces...simply color them in, cut them out, and put them together, and you have 9 paper masks to play with and enjoy. 32pp. 8¼ × 11. 23171-2 Pa. $2.25

A CHRISTMAS CAROL: THE ORIGINAL MANUSCRIPT, Charles Dickens. Clear facsimile of Dickens manuscript, on facing pages with final printed text. 8 illustrations by John Leech, 4 in color on covers. 144pp. 8⅜ × 11¼. 20980-6 Pa. $5.95

CARVING SHOREBIRDS, Harry V. Shourds & Anthony Hillman. 16 full-size patterns (all double-page spreads) for 19 North American shorebirds with step-by-step instructions. 72pp. 9¼ × 12¼. 24287-0 Pa. $4.95

THE GENTLE ART OF MATHEMATICS, Dan Pedoe. Mathematical games, probability, the question of infinity, topology, how the laws of algebra work, problems of irrational numbers, and more. 42 figures. 143pp. 5⅜ × 8½. (EBE) 22949-1 Pa. $3.50

READY-TO-USE DOLLHOUSE WALLPAPER, Katzenbach & Warren, Inc. Stripe, 2 floral stripes, 2 allover florals, polka dot; all in full color. 4 sheets (350 sq. in.) of each, enough for average room. 48pp. 8¼ × 11. 23495-9 Pa. $2.95

MINIATURE IRON-ON TRANSFER PATTERNS FOR DOLLHOUSES, DOLLS, AND SMALL PROJECTS, Rita Weiss and Frank Fontana. Over 100 miniature patterns: rugs, bedspreads, quilts, chair seats, etc. In standard dollhouse size. 48pp. 8¼ × 11. 23741-9 Pa. $1.95

THE DINOSAUR COLORING BOOK, Anthony Rao. 45 renderings of dinosaurs, fossil birds, turtles, other creatures of Mesozoic Era. Scientifically accurate. Captions. 48pp. 8¼ × 11. 24022-3 Pa. $2.25

JAPANESE DESIGN MOTIFS, Matsuya Co. Mon, or heraldic designs. Over 4000 typical, beautiful designs: birds, animals, flowers, swords, fans, geometrics; all beautifully stylized. 213pp. 11⅜ × 8¼. 22874-6 Pa. $7.95

THE TALE OF BENJAMIN BUNNY, Beatrix Potter. Peter Rabbit's cousin coaxes him back into Mr. McGregor's garden for a whole new set of adventures. All 27 full-color illustrations. 59pp. 4¼ × 5½. (Available in U.S. only) 21102-9 Pa. $1.50

THE TALE OF PETER RABBIT AND OTHER FAVORITE STORIES BOXED SET, Beatrix Potter. Seven of Beatrix Potter's best-loved tales including Peter Rabbit in a specially designed, durable boxed set. 4¼ × 5½. Total of 447pp. 158 color illustrations. (Available in U.S. only) 23903-9 Pa. $10.80

PRACTICAL MENTAL MAGIC, Theodore Annemann. Nearly 200 astonishing feats of mental magic revealed in step-by-step detail. Complete advice on staging, patter, etc. Illustrated. 320pp. 5⅜ × 8½. 24426-1 Pa. $5.95

CELEBRATED CASES OF JUDGE DEE (DEE GOONG AN), translated by Robert Van Gulik. Authentic 18th-century Chinese detective novel; Dee and associates solve three interlocked cases. Led to van Gulik's own stories with same characters. Extensive introduction. 9 illustrations. 237pp. 5⅜ × 8½. 23337-5 Pa. $4.50

CUT & FOLD EXTRATERRESTRIAL INVADERS THAT FLY, M. Grater. Stage your own lilliputian space battles.By following the step-by-step instructions and explanatory diagrams you can launch 22 full-color fliers into space. 36pp. 8¼ × 11. 24478-4 Pa. $2.95

CUT & ASSEMBLE VICTORIAN HOUSES, Edmund V. Gillon, Jr. Printed in full color on heavy cardboard stock, 4 authentic Victorian houses in H-O scale: Italian-style Villa, Octagon, Second Empire, Stick Style. 48pp. 9¼ × 12¼. 23849-0 Pa. $3.95

BEST SCIENCE FICTION STORIES OF H.G. WELLS, H.G. Wells. Full novel *The Invisible Man*, plus 17 short stories: "The Crystal Egg," "Aepyornis Island," "The Strange Orchid," etc. 303pp. 5⅜ × 8½. (Available in U.S. only) 21531-8 Pa. $4.95

TRADEMARK DESIGNS OF THE WORLD, Yusaku Kamekura. A lavish collection of nearly 700 trademarks, the work of Wright, Loewy, Klee, Binder, hundreds of others. 160pp. 8¾ × 8. (Available in U.S. only) 24191-2 Pa. $5.00

THE ARTIST'S AND CRAFTSMAN'S GUIDE TO REDUCING, ENLARGING AND TRANSFERRING DESIGNS, Rita Weiss. Discover, reduce, enlarge, transfer designs from any objects to any craft project. 12pp. plus 16 sheets special graph paper. 8¼ × 11. 24142-4 Pa. $3.25

TREASURY OF JAPANESE DESIGNS AND MOTIFS FOR ARTISTS AND CRAFTSMEN, edited by Carol Belanger Grafton. Indispensable collection of 360 traditional Japanese designs and motifs redrawn in clean, crisp black-and-white, copyright-free illustrations. 96pp. 8¼ × 11. 24435-0 Pa. $3.95

CHANCERY CURSIVE STROKE BY STROKE, Arthur Baker. Instructions and illustrations for each stroke of each letter (upper and lower case) and numerals. 54 full-page plates. 64pp. 8¼ × 11. 24278-1 Pa. $2.50

THE ENJOYMENT AND USE OF COLOR, Walter Sargent. Color relationships, values, intensities; complementary colors, illumination, similar topics. Color in nature and art. 7 color plates, 29 illustrations. 274pp. 5⅜ × 8½. 20944-X Pa. $4.50

SCULPTURE PRINCIPLES AND PRACTICE, Louis Slobodkin. Step-by-step approach to clay, plaster, metals, stone; classical and modern. 253 drawings, photos. 255pp. 8⅛ × 11. 22960-2 Pa. $7.50

VICTORIAN FASHION PAPER DOLLS FROM HARPER'S BAZAR, 1867-1898, Theodore Menten. Four female dolls with 28 elegant high fashion costumes, printed in full color. 32pp. 9¼ × 12¼. 23453-3 Pa. $3.50

FLOPSY, MOPSY AND COTTONTAIL: A Little Book of Paper Dolls in Full Color, Susan LaBelle. Three dolls and 21 costumes (7 for each doll) show Peter Rabbit's siblings dressed for holidays, gardening, hiking, etc. Charming borders, captions. 48pp. 4¼ × 5½. 24376-1 Pa. $2.25

NATIONAL LEAGUE BASEBALL CARD CLASSICS, Bert Randolph Sugar. 83 big-leaguers from 1909-69 on facsimile cards. Hubbell, Dean, Spahn, Brock plus advertising, info, no duplications. Perforated, detachable. 16pp. 8¼ × 11. 24308-7 Pa. $2.95

THE LOGICAL APPROACH TO CHESS, Dr. Max Euwe, et al. First-rate text of comprehensive strategy, tactics, theory for the amateur. No gambits to memorize, just a clear, logical approach. 224pp. 5⅜ × 8½. 24353-2 Pa. $4.50

MAGICK IN THEORY AND PRACTICE, Aleister Crowley. The summation of the thought and practice of the century's most famous necromancer, long hard to find. Crowley's best book. 436pp. 5⅜ × 8½. (Available in U.S. only) 23295-6 Pa. $6.50

THE HAUNTED HOTEL, Wilkie Collins. Collins' last great tale; doom and destiny in a Venetian palace. Praised by T.S. Eliot. 127pp. 5⅜ × 8½. 24333-8 Pa. $3.00

ART DECO DISPLAY ALPHABETS, Dan X. Solo. Wide variety of bold yet elegant lettering in handsome Art Deco styles. 100 complete fonts, with numerals, punctuation, more. 104pp. 8⅛ × 11. 24372-9 Pa. $4.00

CALLIGRAPHIC ALPHABETS, Arthur Baker. Nearly 150 complete alphabets by outstanding contemporary. Stimulating ideas; useful source for unique effects. 154 plates. 157pp. 8⅜ × 11¼. 21045-6 Pa. $4.95

ARTHUR BAKER'S HISTORIC CALLIGRAPHIC ALPHABETS, Arthur Baker. From monumental capitals of first-century Rome to humanistic cursive of 16th century, 33 alphabets in fresh interpretations. 88 plates. 96pp. 9 × 12. 24054-1 Pa. $4.50

LETTIE LANE PAPER DOLLS, Sheila Young. Genteel turn-of-the-century family very popular then and now. 24 paper dolls. 16 plates in full color. 32pp. 9¼ × 12¼. 24089-4 Pa. $3.50

KEYBOARD WORKS FOR SOLO INSTRUMENTS, G.F. Handel. 35 neglected works from Handel's vast oeuvre, originally jotted down as improvisations. Includes Eight Great Suites, others. New sequence. 174pp. 9⅜ × 12¼.

24338-9 Pa. $7.50

AMERICAN LEAGUE BASEBALL CARD CLASSICS, Bert Randolph Sugar. 82 stars from 1900s to 60s on facsimile cards. Ruth, Cobb, Mantle, Williams, plus advertising, info, no duplications. Perforated, detachable. 16pp. 8¼ × 11.

24286-2 Pa. $2.95

A TREASURY OF CHARTED DESIGNS FOR NEEDLEWORKERS, Georgia Gorham and Jeanne Warth. 141 charted designs: owl, cat with yarn, tulips, piano, spinning wheel, covered bridge, Victorian house and many others. 48pp. 8¼ × 11.

23558-0 Pa. $1.95

DANISH FLORAL CHARTED DESIGNS, Gerda Bengtsson. Exquisite collection of over 40 different florals: anemone, Iceland poppy, wild fruit, pansies, many others. 45 illustrations. 48pp. 8¼ × 11.
23957-8 Pa. $1.75

OLD PHILADELPHIA IN EARLY PHOTOGRAPHS 1839-1914, Robert F. Looney. 215 photographs: panoramas, street scenes, landmarks, President-elect Lincoln's visit, 1876 Centennial Exposition, much more. 230pp. 8⅜ × 11¾.

23345-6 Pa. $9.95

PRELUDE TO MATHEMATICS, W.W. Sawyer. Noted mathematician's lively, stimulating account of non-Euclidean geometry, matrices, determinants, group theory, other topics. Emphasis on novel, striking aspects. 224pp. 5⅜ × 8½.

24401-6 Pa. $4.50

ADVENTURES WITH A MICROSCOPE, Richard Headstrom. 59 adventures with clothing fibers, protozoa, ferns and lichens, roots and leaves, much more. 142 illustrations. 232pp. 5⅜ × 8½.   23471-1 Pa. $3.95

IDENTIFYING ANIMAL TRACKS: MAMMALS, BIRDS, AND OTHER ANIMALS OF THE EASTERN UNITED STATES, Richard Headstrom. For hunters, naturalists, scouts, nature-lovers. Diagrams of tracks, tips on identification. 128pp. 5⅜ × 8.   24442-3 Pa. $3.50

VICTORIAN FASHIONS AND COSTUMES FROM HARPER'S BAZAR, 1867-1898, edited by Stella Blum. Day costumes, evening wear, sports clothes, shoes, hats, other accessories in over 1,000 detailed engravings. 320pp. 9⅜ × 12¼.

22990-4 Pa. $9.95

EVERYDAY FASHIONS OF THE TWENTIES AS PICTURED IN SEARS AND OTHER CATALOGS, edited by Stella Blum. Actual dress of the Roaring Twenties, with text by Stella Blum. Over 750 illustrations, captions. 156pp. 9 × 12.

24134-3 Pa. $8.50

HALL OF FAME BASEBALL CARDS, edited by Bert Randolph Sugar. Cy Young, Ted Williams, Lou Gehrig, and many other Hall of Fame greats on 92 full-color, detachable reprints of early baseball cards. No duplication of cards with *Classic Baseball Cards.* 16pp. 8¼ × 11.   23624-2 Pa. $3.50

THE ART OF HAND LETTERING, Helm Wotzkow. Course in hand lettering, Roman, Gothic, Italic, Block, Script. Tools, proportions, optical aspects, individual variation. Very quality conscious. Hundreds of specimens. 320pp. 5⅜ × 8½.

21797-3 Pa. $4.95

HOW THE OTHER HALF LIVES, Jacob A. Riis. Journalistic record of filth, degradation, upward drive in New York immigrant slums, shops, around 1900. New edition includes 100 original Riis photos, monuments of early photography. 233pp. 10 × 7⅞. 22012-5 Pa. $7.95

CHINA AND ITS PEOPLE IN EARLY PHOTOGRAPHS, John Thomson. In 200 black-and-white photographs of exceptional quality photographic pioneer Thomson captures the mountains, dwellings, monuments and people of 19th-century China. 272pp. 9⅜ × 12¼. 24393-1 Pa. $12.95

GODEY COSTUME PLATES IN COLOR FOR DECOUPAGE AND FRAMING, edited by Eleanor Hasbrouk Rawlings. 24 full-color engravings depicting 19th-century Parisian haute couture. Printed on one side only. 56pp. 8¼ × 11. 23879-2 Pa. $3.95

ART NOUVEAU STAINED GLASS PATTERN BOOK, Ed Sibbett, Jr. 104 projects using well-known themes of Art Nouveau: swirling forms, florals, peacocks, and sensuous women. 60pp. 8¼ × 11. 23577-7 Pa. $3.50

QUICK AND EASY PATCHWORK ON THE SEWING MACHINE: Susan Aylsworth Murwin and Suzzy Payne. Instructions, diagrams show exactly how to machine sew 12 quilts. 48pp. of templates. 50 figures. 80pp. 8¼ × 11. 23770-2 Pa. $3.50

THE STANDARD BOOK OF QUILT MAKING AND COLLECTING, Marguerite Ickis. Full information, full-sized patterns for making 46 traditional quilts, also 150 other patterns. 483 illustrations. 273pp. 6⅞ × 9⅝. 20582-7 Pa. $5.95

LETTERING AND ALPHABETS, J. Albert Cavanagh. 85 complete alphabets lettered in various styles; instructions for spacing, roughs, brushwork. 121pp. 8¾ × 8. 20053-1 Pa. $3.75

LETTER FORMS: 110 COMPLETE ALPHABETS, Frederick Lambert. 110 sets of capital letters; 16 lower case alphabets; 70 sets of numbers and other symbols. 110pp. 8⅛ × 11. 22872-X Pa. $4.50

ORCHIDS AS HOUSE PLANTS, Rebecca Tyson Northen. Grow cattleyas and many other kinds of orchids—in a window, in a case, or under artificial light. 63 illustrations. 148pp. 5⅜ × 8½. 23261-1 Pa. $2.95

THE MUSHROOM HANDBOOK, Louis C.C. Krieger. Still the best popular handbook. Full descriptions of 259 species, extremely thorough text, poisons, folklore, etc. 32 color plates; 126 other illustrations. 560pp. 5⅜ × 8½. 21861-9 Pa. $8.50

THE DORÉ BIBLE ILLUSTRATIONS, Gustave Doré. All wonderful, detailed plates: Adam and Eve, Flood, Babylon, life of Jesus, etc. Brief King James text with each plate. 241 plates. 241pp. 9 × 12. 23004-X Pa. $8.95

THE BOOK OF KELLS: Selected Plates in Full Color, edited by Blanche Cirker. 32 full-page plates from greatest manuscript-icon of early Middle Ages. Fantastic, mysterious. Publisher's Note. Captions. 32pp. 9¾ × 12¼. 24345-1 Pa. $4.50

THE PERFECT WAGNERITE, George Bernard Shaw. Brilliant criticism of the Ring Cycle, with provocative interpretation of politics, economic theories behind the Ring. 136pp. 5⅜ × 8½. (Available in U.S. only) 21707-8 Pa. $3.00

THE RIME OF THE ANCIENT MARINER, Gustave Doré, S.T. Coleridge. Doré's finest work, 34 plates capture moods, subtleties of poem. Full text. 77pp. 9¼ × 12. 22305-1 Pa. $4.95

SONGS OF INNOCENCE, William Blake. The first and most popular of Blake's famous "Illuminated Books," in a facsimile edition reproducing all 31 brightly colored plates. Additional printed text of each poem. 64pp. 5¼ × 7. 22764-2 Pa. $3.00

AN INTRODUCTION TO INFORMATION THEORY, J.R. Pierce. Second (1980) edition of most impressive non-technical account available. Encoding, entropy, noisy channel, related areas, etc. 320pp. 5⅜ × 8½. 24061-4 Pa. $4.95

THE DIVINE PROPORTION: A STUDY IN MATHEMATICAL BEAUTY, H.E. Huntley. "Divine proportion" or "golden ratio" in poetry, Pascal's triangle, philosophy, psychology, music, mathematical figures, etc. Excellent bridge between science and art. 58 figures. 185pp. 5⅜ × 8½. 22254-3 Pa. $3.95

THE DOVER NEW YORK WALKING GUIDE: From the Battery to Wall Street, Mary J. Shapiro. Superb inexpensive guide to historic buildings and locales in lower Manhattan: Trinity Church, Bowling Green, more. Complete Text; maps. 36 illustrations. 48pp. 3⅞ × 9¼. 24225-0 Pa. $2.50

NEW YORK THEN AND NOW, Edward B. Watson, Edmund V. Gillon, Jr. 83 important Manhattan sites: on facing pages early photographs (1875-1925) and 1976 photos by Gillon. 172 illustrations. 171pp. 9¼ × 10. 23361-8 Pa. $7.95

HISTORIC COSTUME IN PICTURES, Braun & Schneider. Over 1450 costumed figures from dawn of civilization to end of 19th century. English captions. 125 plates. 256pp. 8⅜ × 11¼. 23150-X Pa. $7.50

VICTORIAN AND EDWARDIAN FASHION: A Photographic Survey, Alison Gernsheim. First fashion history completely illustrated by contemporary photographs. Full text plus 235 photos, 1840-1914, in which many celebrities appear. 240pp. 6½ × 9¼. 24205-6 Pa. $6.00

CHARTED CHRISTMAS DESIGNS FOR COUNTED CROSS-STITCH AND OTHER NEEDLECRAFTS, Lindberg Press. Charted designs for 45 beautiful needlecraft projects with many yuletide and wintertime motifs. 48pp. 8¼ × 11. 24356-7 Pa. $1.95

101 FOLK DESIGNS FOR COUNTED CROSS-STITCH AND OTHER NEEDLE-CRAFTS, Carter Houck. 101 authentic charted folk designs in a wide array of lovely representations with many suggestions for effective use. 48pp. 8¼ × 11. 24369-9 Pa. $2.25

FIVE ACRES AND INDEPENDENCE, Maurice G. Kains. Great back-to-the-land classic explains basics of self-sufficient farming. The one book to get. 95 illustrations. 397pp. 5⅜ × 8½. 20974-1 Pa. $4.95

A MODERN HERBAL, Margaret Grieve. Much the fullest, most exact, most useful compilation of herbal material. Gigantic alphabetical encyclopedia, from aconite to zedoary, gives botanical information, medical properties, folklore, economic uses, and much else. Indispensable to serious reader. 161 illustrations. 888pp. 6½ × 9¼. (Available in U.S. only) 22798-7, 22799-5 Pa., Two-vol. set $16.45

DECORATIVE NAPKIN FOLDING FOR BEGINNERS, Lillian Oppenheimer and Natalie Epstein. 22 different napkin folds in the shape of a heart, clown's hat, love knot, etc. 63 drawings. 48pp. 8¼ × 11. 23797-4 Pa. $1.95

DECORATIVE LABELS FOR HOME CANNING, PRESERVING, AND OTHER HOUSEHOLD AND GIFT USES, Theodore Menten. 128 gummed, perforated labels, beautifully printed in 2 colors. 12 versions. Adhere to metal, glass, wood, ceramics. 24pp. 8¼ × 11. 23219-0 Pa. $2.95

EARLY AMERICAN STENCILS ON WALLS AND FURNITURE, Janet Waring. Thorough coverage of 19th-century folk art: techniques, artifacts, surviving specimens. 166 illustrations, 7 in color. 147pp. of text. 7⅞ × 10¾. 21906-2 Pa. $9.95

AMERICAN ANTIQUE WEATHERVANES, A.B. & W.T. Westervelt. Extensively illustrated 1883 catalog exhibiting over 550 copper weathervanes and finials. Excellent primary source by one of the principal manufacturers. 104pp. 6⅛ × 9¼. 24396-6 Pa. $3.95

ART STUDENTS' ANATOMY, Edmond J. Farris. Long favorite in art schools. Basic elements, common positions, actions. Full text, 158 illustrations. 159pp. 5⅜ × 8½. 20744-7 Pa. $3.95

BRIDGMAN'S LIFE DRAWING, George B. Bridgman. More than 500 drawings and text teach you to abstract the body into its major masses. Also specific areas of anatomy. 192pp. 6½ × 9¼. (EA) 22710-3 Pa. $4.50

COMPLETE PRELUDES AND ETUDES FOR SOLO PIANO, Frederic Chopin. All 26 Preludes, all 27 Etudes by greatest composer of piano music. Authoritative Paderewski edition. 224pp. 9 × 12. (Available in U.S. only) 24052-5 Pa. $7.50

PIANO MUSIC 1888-1905, Claude Debussy. Deux Arabesques, Suite Bergamesque, Masques, 1st series of Images, etc. 9 others, in corrected editions. 175pp. 9⅜ × 12¼. (ECE) 22771-5 Pa. $5.95

TEDDY BEAR IRON-ON TRANSFER PATTERNS, Ted Menten. 80 iron-on transfer patterns of male and female Teddys in a wide variety of activities, poses, sizes. 48pp. 8¼ × 11. 24596-9 Pa. $2.25

A PICTURE HISTORY OF THE BROOKLYN BRIDGE, M.J. Shapiro. Profusely illustrated account of greatest engineering achievement of 19th century. 167 rare photos & engravings recall construction, human drama. Extensive, detailed text. 122pp. 8¼ × 11. 24403-2 Pa. $7.95

NEW YORK IN THE THIRTIES, Berenice Abbott. Noted photographer's fascinating study shows new buildings that have become famous and old sights that have disappeared forever. 97 photographs. 97pp. 11⅜ × 10. 22967-X Pa. $6.50

MATHEMATICAL TABLES AND FORMULAS, Robert D. Carmichael and Edwin R. Smith. Logarithms, sines, tangents, trig functions, powers, roots, reciprocals, exponential and hyperbolic functions, formulas and theorems. 269pp. 5⅜ × 8½. 60111-0 Pa. $3.75

HANDBOOK OF MATHEMATICAL FUNCTIONS WITH FORMULAS, GRAPHS, AND MATHEMATICAL TABLES, edited by Milton Abramowitz and Irene A. Stegun. Vast compendium: 29 sets of tables, some to as high as 20 places. 1,046pp. 8 × 10½. 61272-4 Pa. $19.95

REASON IN ART, George Santayana. Renowned philosopher's provocative, seminal treatment of basis of art in instinct and experience. Volume Four of *The Life of Reason*. 230pp. 5⅜ × 8.   24358-3 Pa. $4.50

LANGUAGE, TRUTH AND LOGIC, Alfred J. Ayer. Famous, clear introduction to Vienna, Cambridge schools of Logical Positivism. Role of philosophy, elimination of metaphysics, nature of analysis, etc. 160pp. 5⅜ × 8½. (USCO)
20010-8 Pa. $2.75

BASIC ELECTRONICS, U.S. Bureau of Naval Personnel. Electron tubes, circuits, antennas, AM, FM, and CW transmission and receiving, etc. 560 illustrations. 567pp. 6½ × 9¼.   21076-6 Pa. $8.95

THE ART DECO STYLE, edited by Theodore Menten. Furniture, jewelry, metalwork, ceramics, fabrics, lighting fixtures, interior decors, exteriors, graphics from pure French sources. Over 400 photographs. 183pp. 8⅜ × 11¼.
22824-X Pa. $6.95

THE FOUR BOOKS OF ARCHITECTURE, Andrea Palladio. 16th-century classic covers classical architectural remains, Renaissance revivals, classical orders, etc. 1738 Ware English edition. 216 plates. 110pp. of text. 9½ × 12¾.
21308-0 Pa. $11.50

THE WIT AND HUMOR OF OSCAR WILDE, edited by Alvin Redman. More than 1000 ripostes, paradoxes, wisecracks: Work is the curse of the drinking classes, I can resist everything except temptations, etc. 258pp. 5⅜ × 8½. (USCO)
20602-5 Pa. $3.50

THE DEVIL'S DICTIONARY, Ambrose Bierce. Barbed, bitter, brilliant witticisms in the form of a dictionary. Best, most ferocious satire America has produced. 145pp. 5⅜ × 8½.   20487-1 Pa. $2.50

ERTÉ'S FASHION DESIGNS, Erté. 210 black-and-white inventions from *Harper's Bazar*, 1918-32, plus 8pp. full-color covers. Captions. 88pp. 9 × 12.
24203-X Pa. $6.50

ERTÉ GRAPHICS, Erté. Collection of striking color graphics: *Seasons, Alphabet, Numerals, Aces* and *Precious Stones*. 50 plates, including 4 on covers. 48pp. 9⅜ × 12¼.   23580-7 Pa. $6.95

PAPER FOLDING FOR BEGINNERS, William D. Murray and Francis J. Rigney. Clearest book for making origami sail boats, roosters, frogs that move legs, etc. 40 projects. More than 275 illustrations. 94pp. 5⅜ × 8½.   20713-7 Pa. $2.25

ORIGAMI FOR THE ENTHUSIAST, John Montroll. Fish, ostrich, peacock, squirrel, rhinoceros, Pegasus, 19 other intricate subjects. Instructions. Diagrams. 128pp. 9 × 12.   23799-0 Pa. $4.95

CROCHETING NOVELTY POT HOLDERS, edited by Linda Macho. 64 useful, whimsical pot holders feature kitchen themes, animals, flowers, other novelties. Surprisingly easy to crochet. Complete instructions. 48pp. 8¼ × 11.
24296-X Pa. $1.95

CROCHETING DOILIES, edited by Rita Weiss. Irish Crochet, Jewel, Star Wheel, Vanity Fair and more. Also luncheon and console sets, runners and centerpieces. 51 illustrations. 48pp. 8¼ × 11.   23424-X Pa. $2.00

YUCATAN BEFORE AND AFTER THE CONQUEST, Diego de Landa. Only significant account of Yucatan written in the early post-Conquest era. Translated by William Gates. Over 120 illustrations. 162pp. 5⅜ × 8½.   23622-6 Pa. $3.50

ORNATE PICTORIAL CALLIGRAPHY, E.A. Lupfer. Complete instructions, over 150 examples help you create magnificent "flourishes" from which beautiful animals and objects gracefully emerge. 8⅛ × 11.   21957-7 Pa. $2.95

DOLLY DINGLE PAPER DOLLS, Grace Drayton. Cute chubby children by same artist who did Campbell Kids. Rare plates from 1910s. 30 paper dolls and over 100 outfits reproduced in full color. 32pp. 9¼ × 12¼.   23711-7 Pa. $3.50

CURIOUS GEORGE PAPER DOLLS IN FULL COLOR, H. A. Rey, Kathy Allert. Naughty little monkey-hero of children's books in two doll figures, plus 48 full-color costumes: pirate, Indian chief, fireman, more. 32pp. 9¼ × 12¼.
24386-9 Pa. $3.50

GERMAN: HOW TO SPEAK AND WRITE IT, Joseph Rosenberg. Like *French, How to Speak and Write It.* Very rich modern course, with a wealth of pictorial material. 330 illustrations. 384pp. 5⅜ × 8½. (USUKO)   20271-2 Pa. $4.75

CATS AND KITTENS: 24 Ready-to-Mail Color Photo Postcards, D. Holby. Handsome collection; feline in a variety of adorable poses. Identifications. 12pp. on postcard stock. 8¼ × 11.   24469-5 Pa. $2.95

MARILYN MONROE PAPER DOLLS, Tom Tierney. 31 full-color designs on heavy stock, from *The Asphalt Jungle,Gentlemen Prefer Blondes*, 22 others. 1 doll. 16 plates. 32pp. 9⅜ × 12¼.   23769-9 Pa. $3.50

FUNDAMENTALS OF LAYOUT, F.H. Wills. All phases of layout design discussed and illustrated in 121 illustrations. Indispensable as student's text or handbook for professional. 124pp. 8⅛.× 11.   21279-3 Pa. $4.50

FANTASTIC SUPER STICKERS, Ed Sibbett, Jr. 75 colorful pressure-sensitive stickers. Peel off and place for a touch of pizzazz: clowns, penguins, teddy bears, etc. Full color. 16pp. 8¼ × 11.   24471-7 Pa. $2.95

LABELS FOR ALL OCCASIONS, Ed Sibbett, Jr. 6 labels each of 16 different designs—baroque, art nouveau, art deco, Pennsylvania Dutch, etc.—in full color. 24pp. 8¼ × 11.   23688-9 Pa. $2.95

HOW TO CALCULATE QUICKLY: RAPID METHODS IN BASIC MATHE-MATICS, Henry Sticker. Addition, subtraction, multiplication, division, checks, etc. More than 8000 problems, solutions. 185pp. 5 × 7¼.   20295-X Pa. $2.95

THE CAT COLORING BOOK, Karen Baldauski. Handsome, realistic renderings of 40 splendid felines, from American shorthair to exotic types. 44 plates. Captions. 48pp. 8¼ × 11.   24011-8 Pa. $2.25

THE TALE OF PETER RABBIT, Beatrix Potter. The inimitable Peter's terrifying adventure in Mr. McGregor's garden, with all 27 wonderful, full-color Potter illustrations. 55pp. 4¼ × 5½. (Available in U.S. only)   22827-4 Pa. $1.60

BASIC ELECTRICITY, U.S. Bureau of Naval Personnel. Batteries, circuits, conductors, AC and DC, inductance and capacitance, generators, motors, transformers, amplifiers, etc. 349 illustrations. 448pp. 6½ × 9¼.   20973-3 Pa. $7.95

CATALOG OF DOVER BOOKS

SOURCE BOOK OF MEDICAL HISTORY, edited by Logan Clendening, M.D. Original accounts ranging from Ancient Egypt and Greece to discovery of X-rays: Galen, Pasteur, Lavoisier, Harvey, Parkinson, others. 685pp. 5⅜ × 8½.
20621-1 Pa. $10.95

THE ROSE AND THE KEY, J.S. Lefanu. Superb mystery novel from Irish master. Dark doings among an ancient and aristocratic English family. Well-drawn characters; capital suspense. Introduction by N. Donaldson. 448pp. 5⅜ × 8½.
24377-X Pa. $6.95

SOUTH WIND, Norman Douglas. Witty, elegant novel of ideas set on languorous Mediterranean island of Nepenthe. Elegant prose, glittering epigrams, mordant satire. 1917 masterpiece. 416pp. 5⅜ × 8½. (Available in U.S. only)
24361-3 Pa. $5.95

RUSSELL'S CIVIL WAR PHOTOGRAPHS, Capt. A.J. Russell. 116 rare Civil War Photos: Bull Run, Virginia campaigns, bridges, railroads, Richmond, Lincoln's funeral car. Many never seen before. Captions. 128pp. 9⅜ × 12¼.
24283-8 Pa. $6.95

PHOTOGRAPHS BY MAN RAY: 105 Works, 1920-1934. Nudes, still lifes, landscapes, women's faces, celebrity portraits (Dali, Matisse, Picasso, others), rayographs. Reprinted from rare gravure edition. 128pp. 9⅜ × 12¼. (Available in U.S. only)
23842-3 Pa. $6.95

STAR NAMES: THEIR LORE AND MEANING, Richard H. Allen. Star names, the zodiac, constellations: folklore and literature associated with heavens. The basic book of its field, fascinating reading. 563pp. 5⅜ × 8½.
21079-0 Pa. $7.95

BURNHAM'S CELESTIAL HANDBOOK, Robert Burnham, Jr. Thorough guide to the stars beyond our solar system. Exhaustive treatment. Alphabetical by constellation: Andromeda to Cetus in Vol. 1; Chamaeleon to Orion in Vol. 2; and Pavo to Vulpecula in Vol. 3. Hundreds of illustrations. Index in Vol. 3. 2000pp. 6⅛ × 9¼.
23567-X, 23568-8, 23673-0 Pa. Three-vol. set $36.85

THE ART NOUVEAU STYLE BOOK OF ALPHONSE MUCHA, Alphonse Mucha. All 72 plates from *Documents Decoratifs* in original color. Stunning, essential work of Art Nouveau. 80pp. 9⅜ × 12¼.
24044-4 Pa. $7.95

DESIGNS BY ERTE; FASHION DRAWINGS AND ILLUSTRATIONS FROM "HARPER'S BAZAR," Erte. 310 fabulous line drawings and 14 *Harper's Bazar* covers, 8 in full color. Erte's exotic temptresses with tassels, fur muffs, long trains, coifs, more. 129pp. 9⅜ × 12¼.
23397-9 Pa. $6.95

HISTORY OF STRENGTH OF MATERIALS, Stephen P. Timoshenko. Excellent historical survey of the strength of materials with many references to the theories of elasticity and structure. 245 figures. 452pp. 5⅜ × 8½. 61187-6 Pa. $8.95

Prices subject to change without notice.
Available at your book dealer or write for free catalog to Dept. GI, Dover Publications, Inc., 31 East 2nd St. Mineola, N.Y. 11501. Dover publishes more than 175 books each year on science, elementary and advanced mathematics, biology, music, art, literary history, social sciences and other areas.